Stress Test for Democracy

How Social Media Undermine Social Peace

Marc Nottelmann-Feil

Stress Test for Democracy

How Social Media Undermine Social Peace

Marc Nottelmann-Feil read Japanese Studies, Mathematics, Logic and Philosophy of Science. Since 2000 he has been working for the "EKO House of Japanese Culture" in Duesseldorf. He is a Buddhist priest of the Jodo Shinshu school.

Bibliographical Information of the German National Library:

German National Library Cataloguing available in the Germany National Bibliography. For detailed bibliographical information visit http://dnb.dnb.de on the Internet.

© 2018 Marc Nottelmann-Feil

Original: "Demokratie im Stresstest", 8 May 2017

Translation: Sabine Reinhold

Printed and published by BoD – Books on Demand, Norderstedt

ISBN: 978-3-7481-4859-3

Table of Contents

Introduction 7

Beware of E-Mails! 13

Facebook or the Invention of Synthetic Mass Communication 29

The Arsonists 37

The Structure of So-Called Conversations 43

#ScrewtheEstablishment! 55

Opinion-Forming in the Virtual Society 65

From Clear-Cut Front Lines to Civil War 75

Twitter - Leading Opinion Through Self- Advertising 87

What is truth, Mr Pilatus? 97

Humans and the Vision of Humanity in the Social Media 103

First-Aid Measures and Wrong Expectations 115

Peace With Facebook & Co? 123

On A Final Note 131

Recommended Literature 135

Introduction

There are years in which history seems to pick up speed. Old political structures long considered as rock-solid and unassailable suddenly break apart to be replaced by something new, but nobody knows what it will be. Since 2011 the tides in the world have been turning: the Middle East is burning, the EU is disintegrating, Russia has returned to its expansion politics inspired by geopolitical thinking, and the United States of America have elected a president who places his country's interests above all else.

The West is still at the helm. But when one takes a step back to look at the whole picture, ignoring small details to get only the rough outlines, it is, after all, the vision of humanity developed in Western philosophy that is at work behind all these phenomena. The human being is considered as a creature driven by greed that fights against its fellows to satisfy its personal interests. Competition rules all walks of life, including states and worldwide business. Nothing is more important - for the individual as well as nations - than moving on as fast a possible; any opportunity for profit must be identified as early as possible and used ruthlessly, at the expense of the slower moving or more circumspect, where necessary. This attitude leads to deregulation, more free trade at all costs, to the careless consumption of our world's finite resources, and to the increasingly painful gap between the rich and the poor. Ultimately, most, if not all, problems that have led up to the described transformations start with the vision of humanity outlined above.

I do not wish to explain why the world is in crisis, though. The questions I have take a different approach: Why are we unable to engage in a social discourse that allows us to find sensible answers to those challenges, although the methods of communication have improved in recent years by all but a quantum leap? Social media are connecting the whole world: never was it easier to make connections, get information about current problems and discussions in even the remotest part of the planet and chime in everywhere. Why are humans incapable of talking to each other and working together towards finding solutions? Any person in Germany with an interest in Ugandan politics can effortlessly stay on top of things: they can learn to understand the thoughts of both government and opposition and tweet or post their own thoughts, almost as if they actually lived in Uganda. When has there ever been such totally unlimited, unfettered freedom! In like manner, all political parties and media in Germany, even the smallest political societies, have web pages on the Internet and German citizens can reach every member of the Bundestag with just a few mouse clicks, seeming to put grass-roots democracy within easy reach - yet this fact does not appear to make our society more content or balanced. Quite the contrary: there are burning issues at every turn. Only recently, in his parting speech, German President Joachim Gauck even said that democracy was threatened.[1] Only two years earlier, the great majority of Germans would have considered theirs as one of the most stable democracies in the whole world.

Aren't we getting the basics all wrong? The social media are connecting people around the world, making society move closer together - that is our first, seemingly positive impression. The reality we are witnessing, however, is totally different: Since the launch of Facebook (2004) and Twitter (2006), political structures have been disintegrating: The Arab Spring (2011) - applauded by the West for toppling Arab autocracies - started in one of the Internet cafés of Tunis and Cairo. For a moment it seemed as if Western Enlightenment, following the eternal laws of history, would prevail over Eastern tyranny: the impoverished peoples of North Africa rose up against their corrupt elites. However, the Arab Spring was not followed by an era of Arab Reason but by a power vacuum exposing the various societies' inner conflicts even more clearly, causing them to erupt

---

[1] Joachim Gauck's parting speech of January 17, 2017.

into disastrous civil wars. Why were the social media capable of shaking up the political structures of these countries, but failed to provide the social glue of solidarity? Why have these countries, to this day, not found their way back to peace, although Facebook could make it so easy to talk to enemies - unencumbered by international diplomacy and laboriously arranged peace conferences? It seems that the social media may be able to stir up a society but lack the power to bring about a process of social healing.

In 2016, the wave of disruption associated so closely with social media finally reached Western countries and societies. Events occurred that neither pollsters nor established media had predicted or reckoned with. Both the Brexit as well as the election of Donald Trump to President of the United States struck the world like lightning out of the blue, because the established media - television, press, and radio - continued to do their job the way they had always done it: they published reports about party conventions, held talk shows with varying participants, but failed to take notice of the semi-public sectors (plural!) inhabiting in the social media. Periodicals like the "Guardian" or the "New York Times" revelled in the illusion that they were the undisputed opinion leaders and that the opinions discussed in the social media would therefore follow their lead. But social media follow different laws, that much should be clear by now. Donald Trump managed to prevail over the combined power of the established media by means of Twitter and lowbrow TV shows. The ensuing shock waves running through the most powerful democracy of the world are an eye-opener to how ruthless a catalyst for disruption the social media are.

So, we should stop whitewashing social media as a means of non-hierarchical discourse, as a trailblazer for grass-roots democracy or as a tool for educating people and public! Instead, we should start to explore how they actually work and what impact their use has on society. Finally, we should ponder the question what we want our future life with these social media to look like, or in other words, how they and we have to change so life in this new situation will be possible.

Beware of E-Mails!

The human being is a creature that can abruptly change its communication patterns. There is no such thing as community without communication, whereas communication without community is quite possible. At the beginnings of our history as humans, communication and community were almost identical: Community was social interaction that provided the setting for communication. In a small group of hunters and gatherers, every one knows every one else, each individual knows many things about his or her fellows and there are hardly any secrets between the group members. Every communication is essentially public, like the hunting bag, that is publicly divided up between the community members. Later, as those communities grew larger, it soon became impossible to know every member of the group. This lead to the development of an increasingly complex role distribution defining who was in charge of what situation. New forms of exchange emerged: the messenger, the written word, letters, the printing press, etc - each of which completely changed the communication patterns of society. Communication became more abstract and less dependent on direct interaction between humans. When using the modern-day media that developed over the past hundred years, when writing a letter or reading a book, we are performing a communicative act even though we may feel terribly lonely in the process.

The emergence of new communication methods in times of radical technological change is neither surprising nor a bad thing in itself. Yet, any novelty also requires increased attention. As long as its significance is not fully understood, this novelty will pose a threat, because it is considered to be no more than a playful continuation of something old. There is a critical phase in which people stick to their set ways while the novelty appears in the guise of the familiar. People tinker and ponder, they are willing to make some, though clearly limited, space for the novelty, assuming that they will be able to find some arrangement with it. But the novelty does not fit into old moulds, it defies classification; instead, the novelty is strong enough to incorporate old ways. This means the first step to overcoming a crisis caused by innovation is to clearly identify what makes the novelty different from what is familiar.

A good ten years ago I noticed for the first time how tightly communication's success or total failure is linked to the applied medium. Back then I was charged with the task of chairing a small association whose members were scattered over a large geographical area. Due to the long distances, both sides, the association members and I, did not know each other very well. Still, there were several tasks that needed to be completed and on top of that, we needed to develop a concept to shape our association's future. I made an astounding experience during that time: Whenever I wrote e-mails to make suggestions or provide information to my fellow associates, the results were often grievous misunderstandings; some of the e-mail exchanges flew completely off the handle and degraded into mutual accusations, although, from my point of view, I had always made a point of being understanding and diplomatic. However, these problems disappeared invariably the moment I picked up the telephone and talked to the person who had felt slighted. Talking, it took no more than a few minutes to dissolve all tension and overcome mistrust, causing doubts to quickly disappear into thin air. Obviously, the written word was inadequate to pass on information or discuss facts and situations. It was the tone of voice, speaking slowly or rapidly, an approving chuckle or waiting and listening that got communication going and led to a mutually satisfying negotiation outcome. E-mail correspondence often caused both sides to misjudge the weight of a certain statement, causing the reader to assume that the author had ulterior motives - which did not exist - or making the reader feel that he wasn't being taken seriously.

The forwarding of e-mails makes things even worse, because the parties to a conflict always try to gather allies to help them. When you are convinced that you are right and the other person is wrong, it is extremely easy to take a particular passage from an e-mail and - interpreting it your way - forward it to a large group of people you know. For the author of the original e-mail message this procedure has frequently terrible consequences, because he suddenly has to justify himself to people he hadn't even thought of at the time he wrote the e-mail.

E-mail (and its little brother, the almost forgotten fax) was the first faceless and voiceless high-speed communication medium that radically cut off all other forms of non-verbal communication. Another feature setting e-mail apart from its precursors is its completely different management that allows almost endless duplication, forwarding and long-term storage. Woe betide those who fail to grasp the difference between new and old media!

A telephone conversation is a far more natural form of communication, not only because it can convey voice modulations but also because it makes the instant of communication unique. Nobody expects to be confronted with an audio recording of some telephone conversation they have had; at least until recently was something that happened only in rare exceptions. Snail mail may contain information that has been fixed, but unless it's a document from some government authority or an invoice, those letters frequently end up in the bin. Snail-mail administration also requires a lot of effort. E-mail, on the other hand, can be left on the server as long as the user has no reason to the delete it; storage space on a server has virtually no limits and search functions ensure fast retrieval. E-mail messages can be retrieved in no time at all for re-discussion, their contents exactly the same as at the time they were created.

Let us assume you had a bad day because the workman who was supposed to repair your washing machine installed the wrong tube. Although the workman's invoice is already lying on your desk, your washing machine is still leaking water. Before making your complaint to the workman you need to let off some steam and grab the phone to ring a friend. Being listened to by a friend and sharing some bad experiences you two made with workmen helps you to regain your composure. Next, you call the workman and explain the problem to him, using calm and friendly words. If you had written two e-mails - instead of making phone calls - tone and message would have been totally different and could have placed you in an extremely awkward situation, if the e-mail intended for your friend had accidentally ended up going to the workman. Try and imagine what would happen if you were a prominent politician and your e-mail had arrived on a WikiLeaks server!

The Chamber of Handicrafts would immediately receive statements, copied from your e-mail, along with comments, and a day later you would be able to read articles about your "duplicity" in the yellow press.

People writing e-mail give up control over their written words, and they have to trust the recipients to handle these words like a true trustee would. Phone calls are transitory, e-mails are forever. Any statement made during a phone call can be revised again and again, while the memories of the conversation partners soften it: in hindsight, the involved parties weren't that furious after all (because the solution to the problem had already been devised), the wording may have been a bit unfortunate (the upcoming compromise is already forming), and some of the stuff is no more than a blurry memory (Fortunately! So let's just forget it!) – This has always been our natural way of communicating, and we practise doing it that way all our lives long. E-mail, on the other hand, is a document that won't go away so easily.

DO NOT CONFUSE THE NEW WAYS WITH THE OLD WAYS - that's the core of media competence. Most people, from Jane Doe to Hillary Clinton, believe that an e-mail server is the equivalent of a snail-mailbox that can be locked with a simple mailbox key, namely a password. The snail-mailbox key on the key ring I carry is the most primitive key of all the keys in the bunch; with a little judicious fiddling, I can actually open my mailbox without using its original key. Still, I am not wasting much thought on that because I cannot imagine that anyone would be interested in the usual snail mail I get. What would a thief gain from stealing the balance statements I regularly get from my bank? I would watch my mailbox more closely only if I were a single woman afraid of becoming victim to stalking. Maybe I would have a post office box at the nearest post office.

But should you be equally careless with your e-mail account? We have become more careful in handling the passwords of our private e-mail accounts since we started to do more online shopping and online banking. So I won't need to explain the significance of secure passwords. Yet, it is still the norm to carelessly store several years' worth of e-mails on unencrypted servers that are financed by commercials. The general belief is that large providers have good e-mail encryption, that they have some kind of a safe-deposit locker for our private e-mail and the larger the provider we entrust our e-mail to, the safer we believe the safe-deposit locker to be, just like a big bank. We believe that having a good password is sufficient to protect our e-mail accounts stored on the servers of well-known, globally operating server providers.

It is true that I, as a private person, would hardly be able to hack the servers of Yahoo or Google Mail, especially since their defence mechanisms are getting increasingly complex. Yet, today's hackers may no longer be just clever teenagers who simply want to try a few things; more likely, today's hackers are the security specialists of server providers who have quietly and secretly defected to the dark side. Moles can probably be found in all major companies: who would swear to it that in a company with thousands of employees there isn't one who may be open to bribery? These insiders may pass on crucial passwords without anyone noticing, granting outsiders access to the e-mailboxes of billions of people, as could recently be seen in the case of Yahoo. These intruders can copy all e-mail of up to the last 20 years without the affected billions of people noticing the least bit, because there aren't any crumpled envelopes or blotted or smeared address lines.

It doesn't require a science-fiction author's imagination to see that intelligence agencies can't but love these possibilities of spying on people. What could be closer to their field of operation? Again and again we see that even the Federal Republic of Germany or the state of North-Rhine Westphalia purchases data sets containing strictly confidential banking information. These purchases take place in broad daylight in front of whole the public and may serve a good cause or not.

How many of such data sets get secretly forwarded to corrupt nations without anyone knowing? Is there any other state besides the Federal Republic of Germany that ever admitted engaging in such transactions?

Worse still, when stealing a password fails and the black market has not got any more on offer, there is the possibility of a so-called brute-force attack that checks all possible passwords, like going through each possible combination of a number lock. For this purpose, the NSA has built up incredible computing power, matching that of Google. So, even without knowing all the passwords, the NSA will be able to read anything if they want to. Yet, there is a crucial downside to brute-force attacks: where passwords are complex enough, it will be extremely expensive to crack them, even with this massive computing power.

"So what?" many people will say, "Who wants to shell out lots of money to read my old e-mail that even I no longer care about?" But gaining access to the e-mails of tens of millions of people might be interesting under certain circumstances... Let's assume you are an ambitious politician intending to set up an autocracy in the long term. Also, you have already risen through the ranks to a political office that puts you in close contact with, or even in charge of, an intelligence authority. Your intelligence service now learns that somewhere in the world the administrator passwords of company Y are up for sale, so you seize the opportunity. As long as your haul is still "hot" and nobody has changed the passwords, you download all of your compatriots' e-mail traffic that you can find on company Y's server. Almost all of it is outdated and uninteresting stuff. But like an archaeologist who can piece together a story with finds from a two-thousand-year-old rubbish heap, you can glean valuable information from this digital miscellany of e-mail spam and old, forgotten invoices. - Who made deprecating remarks about the last few years' tax increases? Simply enter the search term "tax" and narrow it down with a couple of other search terms. And voilà, you can print out a nearly complete list of all people who are dissatisfied with taxation. – Next, you use a couple of big-data search methods: some language features are certain to distinguish a typical voter of the Marxist party from a conservative voter: terms like "peace initiative", "homeland", "comrade", "freedom", or "oppression" are used differently by the various voter groups. A brief search run using big-data methods will be enough to create a very precise map of your compatriots' political orientation. – And you are also certain to stumble across a few persons of public interest during your foray into big data. Perfect! Now you know that the archbishop has a new girlfriend. All this information may prove useful one day.

The things that can happen by HANDING OVER ONE CRUCIAL PASSWORD or a single USB stick dwarfs every-thing that even an intelligence agency like the Stasi used to be capable of. It would not have been possible to screen millions of letters simultaneously, and even if it had been possible, there would have been no way to archive the results to as to allow sifting through the en-tire mass of data for specific information so incredibly fast. The dusty Stasi archives may have stored a lot of information considered as incriminating by the former GDR, but by the time the archive registrar had finished the laborious task of retrieving and analysing the files of suspects, the "agitators" were long gone.

Everybody knows that. The progress digitisation has seen in recent years also lead to a quantum leap in sur-veillance. The case of Edward Snowden in 2013 only shows the determination with which even democratic nations use such surveillance methods. Democracies believe they are doing the right thing, because their po-lice force and intelligence services are controlled by the rule of law. This means that according to their belief they use the information only to protect the rights of their citizens, thereby even increasing the security of a state governed by the rule of law. But, is this the whole truth? Even before Edward Snowden disclosed his col-lection of data to the world, there may have been three of his kind forwarding the same collection of data to the intelligence agencies of Russia, China, and North Korea. Who would know? In light of the possibilities provided by present-day technology, it is foolhardy to believe that such data can simply be locked away. How utterly and totally naive to believe that! There is no such thing as a secure system as long as there are human beings guarding its security. Even the large pyramids of Egypt, monuments to an archaic need for security, were robbed by the contemporaries of the people who built them.

For this reason it was criminally negligent of democratic governments to approve as open a communication system as unencrypted e-mail in the first place. This gave rise to the *Bright Net,* which is even far more dangerous to democracy than the rightly criticised Dark Net. Politics made no effort at all to find a middle ground between these two extremes. We would hardly have felt it if the government had neglected the construction of roads and public infrastructure for a couple of years. But neglecting areas forming the technological infrastructure of a country is sending shock waves through all of the democratic world. The current situation is unstable because all the issues urgently in need of regulation remain opaque, with some of these issues not necessarily supposed to be up for public discussion. But, can we trust a government that let decades go by without setting up a safety plan for the personal data of its citizens?

PARANOIA IS A LOUSY COUNSELLOR. The democracies in this world and their intelligence agencies deserve to be given some advance trust. But all that e-mail stored on servers all over the world is a ticking time bomb, especially for democratic politicians. Every person might get discredited among his or her fellows if their e-mail were published. In the current period of transition, dirty election campaigns will become the norm.

True, it is a bit complicated to encrypt e-mails before sending them in order to protect them against unauthorised access while they are on the way (a problem not yet discussed here). On the other hand, unauthorised access for the purpose of digitally screening e-mail stored on servers as described above is relatively easy to prevent. The user only needs to store his e-mail in encrypted form on the server and make sure he is the only one holding the encryption key. When encryption takes place on the server, without the server provider knowing the user's password, the e-mail is secured against access. What's in it for a burglar if he finds only encrypted messages in the safe? Granted, a powerful intelligence agency with a special interest in the e-mail of a particular user may be able to break the encryption of her e-mails using a brute-force attack, but the agency will think twice and determine whether it is worth spending all that money in the first place. Still, screening the e-mail of millions of users for particular keywords will no longer be so easy to do once the e-mail is encrypted, and an autocrat will not be able to print a list of potential public enemies.

There are e-mail service providers with a small staff who offer to encrypt e-mail stored on their server by means of an external password (not known to the server provider). But this service is always subject to a fee, because it cannot be financed through advertising, for obvious reasons. Conversely, providers offering their servers free of charge cannot offer encryption services, because their business model is based precisely on keeping some kind of access to their users' e-mail. For example, if a user were to write an enthusiastic e-mail about the city of Florence on an e-mail server financed by advertising, the user would later frequently get adverts for Italy in his browser. Whether that is useful or not may be up to debate, but it proves that information taken from the author's e-mail was used, meaning his e-mail stored on the sever was not encrypted.

When weighing these values against one another - the protection of democracy against the business interests of various industries - the answer is clear. The government ought to have acted long ago in order to protect citizens against this kind of attack and required them -

for their own benefit - to use encrypted e-mail accounts. But the government did nothing of the sort. This negligence has now made democracy vulnerable to attack, as demonstrated by the presidential race in the US.

In short, if people get into a row, it is not always through their own personal fault. Frequently it is the fault of the medium through which they are communicating. Users first had to learn how to handle e-mail, as they were not familiar with this new form of communication. E-mail is a written, high-speed communication medium coming with previously unimaginable accessibility, but unable to convey non-verbal information like facial expressions and voice modulation. Anyone who ignores these two completely new features characterising this medium may be up for a rude awakening when using e-mail.

Facebook or the Invention of Synthetic Mass Communication

What do things look like in the case of social media? How are social media different from conventional methods of communication such as the traditional media used for disseminating information and political decision-making? What are their dangers?

The original idea behind social media may have been to encourage togetherness by making society more transparent and accessible. Human relationships tend get off to a rocky start. Not everyone is highly skilled in dealing with people, many are stand-offish and diffident. They usually are the wallflowers confined to the sidelines, although they may have much to say to the world. Then, there are many people with a shared interest who may never meet in all their lives. Why not develop a sort of self-promotion catalogue for a small segment of society such as a university, in which every participant can introduce him- or herself and chat about his or her interests and ideas? The start-up difficulties inherent in human communication would be eliminated, or at least the hurdles for making first contact would be lowered. This was the basic idea of Facebook when it was brought to life in 2004 at Harvard University.

The academic world has always had a need for networking among researchers. Consequently, one of the things inspiring Facebook may well have been the printed university's register of persons that listed the contact details and research interests of the various scholars. This list of people filled several volumes and was so heavy and unwieldy that it was available only in university libraries. But it fulfilled an important function, because it enabled scholars who had never met personally before to get in touch by letter, thereby allowing the organisation of scientific symposia.

The early version of Facebook complemented and then supplanted this dusty behemoth from the old days of academic erudition. Although, in the early days, it connected only the members of Harvard University with each other, Facebook was far more than an academic medium. It appealed to students rather than the professors, it was about the discussion of personal matters rather than scientific exchange. Facebook was more than informative, it was *sexy*. It's truly a millennium that separates Facebook from the academic register of persons.

What had happened? Computer storage discs allowed the aggregation of and access to information on a previously unknown scale. Any number of people from everywhere in the world could access a storage disc and store information there. Facebook organised this process in intelligent fashion, and, instead of meticulously editing information to fit into a five-line entry in the register of persons, people could now enter information as text in any length and layout they wished. It was no longer necessary to laboriously look up an address and take a letter to the post office to get in touch with another member of Harvard University. One single friend request was enough and the exchange could start.

ONE OBJECTION IS OBVIOUS, THOUGH: Isn't it a mistake to place Facebook on a par with the traditional academic register of persons? One could argue that Facebook, in terms of scope and purpose, started out as something totally different than a university's printed Who is Who, which really was no more than an extended phone directory. So the answer must be yes and no, revealing for the first time the full extent of the new media's ambiguity. If, after its launch in 2004, Facebook had been restricted to Harvard University for a longer period of time, the university would have had an incontrovertible academic edge over all other universities in the world, because it is quite possible to organise academic exchange via Facebook. Of course, it is easier for students with similar or interconnecting interests to meet at a mass university if a medium like Facebook is available: they can exchange opinions on scientific topics with their fellow academics in no time at all and form research project groups. So this medium can contribute to a considerable speed-up in academic exchange – if it gets consistently used for this purpose.

Yet, confining the medium's use to only academic circles may have been an objective only in the first stage of its development. Mark Zuckerberg, who published the first version, wanted a change of culture at Harvard University, not only within the confines of the scientific community, but in its entire social life. Facebook opened up unconventional paths to meeting people, even meeting Mr or Mrs Right, or simply arranging to meet up with friends to go to a concert. In other words, Facebook was an in-crowd medium. Given the storage capacity of computers, Harvard University was too small an in-crowd, and science took a critical stance towards Facebook, because, in their view, it was too liberal and chaotic: the users' unedited self-promotion, claiming everything and nothing at the same time, runs counter to all scientific customs and traditions. So Facebook's liason with science was soon ended and it moved on to become a medium of pop culture. From today's perspective, a decision of historic magnitude!

If confined to Harvard for a longer period of time, Facebook might have developed into some sort of digital application dossier and match-maker on one of the classiest labour and marriage markets in the world. The Facebook environment would have been optimally suited to the task, because the element of self-marketing is intrinsic to the platform's DNA. Then again, Facebook might well have developed into a genuinely scientific medium.

It is peculiar that Facebook has never really been able to explain who and what it is supposed to be good for and how people should use it. This is a general truth applying to all of today's social media: depending on the kind of user and the way people use them, social media can completely change their character. They are open to many uses, like an umbrella, that provides shelter during a cloudburst, and, turned upside down, can also be used to catch sweets thrown from the floats of a parade.

A fitting analogy for social media could be a large zoo enclosure designed as an animal habitat. Before building such an enclosure, the people responsible have to plan a long time in advance how large any boulders, trees and feeding areas should be and how they should be arranged to meet the future inhabitants' needs in the best possible way. Which areas of the enclosure will be populated by which species? What will terrain-related encounters between the species look like? Is building only one watering place a good idea when a very dominant male is supposed to live in the enclosure? Will it be possible close off part of the enclosure in case the male doesn't fit into the group? Will there be an area where females and their cubs can seek shelter? The zoo keepers take the characteristics of the various species into account and know very well that a planning mistake can have devastating consequences for the animals living in the enclosure. It is not possible either to simply use the enclosure for a species other than the one it was designed for.

This analogy provides a first impression as to how an open platform like social media must be viewed, why they completely change their character depending on user group, ie university students, sales representatives, or mafiosi. It raises awareness and brings up questions concerning the structure of social media: What kind of people populate them in what way? How will crowds as opposed to individuals behave in these virtual rooms as designed there? It is a mistake to believe that social media are not based on any particular vision of humanity. Like the zoo keepers in the analogy, planning ahead for the animals that are supposed to live in the enclosure, the creators of social media have incorporated their vision of humanity into the program. It is their notion of what is typical of the species homo sapiens that is reflected in the form and structure of social media.

Therefore I am asking you: Are today's social media really appropriate to the species homo sapiens? Or is their design so flawed that it is in their very nature to inadvertently provoke the very conflicts and signs of political decay that we are witnessing right now?

The Arsonists

Gottlieb Biedermann, the protagonist from Max Frisch's famous play "The Arsonists" is a good and respectable citizen. One day he reads in the newspaper that his home town is regularly attacked by arsonists. Disguised as hawkers, they rent the attic of a house that they will later set on fire. Biedermann, thoroughly disgusted, has barely put down his newspaper when a homeless man knocks on his door and asks for shelter in his house. Mr Biedermann finds himself unable to turn the insistent fellow away and allows him to stay in the attic. Soon, there are two homeless men living in the attic. Mr Biedermann frequently hears noise and clatter, and the stairwell often smells of petrol. But the two friendly lodgers always succeed in putting Mr Biedermann's mind at rest by acting innocent and treating him like a buddy. In the end, Mr Biedermann even laughs - though uncomfortably - at their brazen jokes that they are actually arsonists. That is because Mr Biedermann keeps clinging to the hope that his two lodgers are his friends and honest people - until disaster strikes as could be expected.

Let's imagine Mr Biedermann lives today, in 2017. He has already read some negative articles about social media. But a colleague at work convinces him that Facebook will help him stay up-to-date on his hobby and meet people sharing his interests. So Mr Biedermann sets up an account with Facebook. He selects a nice profile photo and background image and - knowing he shouldn't disclose too many details about himself - leaves most of the fields concerning his CV, e-mail address, etc, empty. Then he starts looking for people he knows, sends out some 20 friend requests that get accepted and joins a group for, say, freshwater fish-keeping. Mr Biedermann's experience with Facebook is only positive. Since he has made himself at home on Facebook, he has received occasional posts from his friends. His group discusses questions like: Can you feed neon tetras with daphnia? Should you remove some of the plants to allow more light to fall into the aquarium? Under the group's influence, the aquarist's enthusiasm gradually shifts to the cichlids of Lake Malawi, but he perceives his shift in interest as a gain. For him, Facebook is an asset enhancing his quality of life, a new medium like the television set. Reading in the newspaper about problems with social media only makes him shake his head: That people simply can't draw a line between their public and their private lives!

Mr Biedermann does not understand why Facebook is being criticised When used responsibly, so Mr Biedermann believes, Facebook is a completely inoffensive medium. Accusing Facebook of commercialisation seems absurd to him. He knows of course why Facebook shows especially to him so many commercials for fish food. He may also suspect they are trying to steer him towards a more expensive type of fish-keeping (How about saltwater fish-keeping? Aren't the cichlids from Lake Malawi particularly beautiful?) But he puts up with all of that. After all, he is used to passing large advertising billboards on the way to work, usually ignoring them. But these commercials have also given him the odd useful idea. In short, in Mr Biedermann's view Facebook hasn't changed the world that much. To Mr Biedermann the novelty appears in the guise of the familiar.

CHANGE OF SCENE: Other than the fish-keeping group which is concerned only with exchanging factual information, politics is a field of complex reasoning that never leads to clear answers. Let's assume in the second part of our play that Mr Biedermann is interested in politics. A couple of years ago, after careful consideration, he joined in a political party and now regularly visits their local group meetings, eagerly participating in the discussions. Differing opinions clash, although the party members all agree on the party's basic objectives. Mr Biedermann tremendously enjoys the political discourse and wishes to continue it on Facebook. In the beginning, he links up with friends and party colleagues. Up to this point, his Facebook world corresponds to his real-life relationships and Mr Biedermann makes only positive experiences.

But then - we are already in the third scene of our play - Mr Biedermann takes the next step. Facebook has suggested that he join a political group concerned with the issue that was the reason he became involved in politics in the first place. There are already 500 people meeting in an open discussion forum: everyone can post his or her opinion or comment on other people's posts. Mr Biedermann has frequently discussed politics with people of different political orientations. That's normal when he meets people outside his party's conventions, so joining a discussion group that doesn't require him to be a party member is alluring. Mr Biedermann expects to have regular discussions with other citizens. But during his first few sessions he realises that something is different in this group. The atmosphere is more aggressive, many statements are astoundingly biased. That's not how the discussion would go in a local party group, and behaviour in Parliament would be different too. Barbs and jibes are getting fired from every direction. Politicians are discredited with few words, doubting their mental competence, personal integrity, or both. Sometimes people post newspaper articles or news clips, with the accompanying text or comments attacking the newspaper or news station with just as much venom. Such intense and frequently excessive emotions are something Mr Biedermann has not known before. He is bewildered by this.

 So he decides to take the initiative, and writes comments in reply to some posts he finds particularly absurd. But the reply Mr Biedermann gets is not from the author of the post he commented on, it is from a third person who opened a sub-thread, because she was riled by some part of Mr Biedermann's comment. Before Mr Biedermann can formulate a defence against the accusation made in the sub-thread, a fourth person has expressed agreement with the third person by simply posting a puking Smiley. By this time, Mr Biedermann's post has moved out of sight, because other users have commented on the original post as well. That's the reason why the users joining the thread later don't even get to see Mr Biedermann's comment, unless they are interested in what is being discussed on the thread and click the "View more" button. In effect, Mr Biedermann's post has all but disappeared from the public. The original post keeps collecting *Likes*, similar opinions keep popping up on the first level of its thread; soon another post appears at the top level of the thread and pushes the older post down on the scroll bar, This post is fresh, so it ousts the previous one.

Mr Biedermann has achieved nothing. His voice hasn't been heard at all. His message has appeared on the screen for three minutes and two total strangers have listened with only half an ear, obviously misunderstanding him. Should Mr Biedermann give up, frustrated? Should he change to another group?

In the theatre play by Max Frisch, the crucial mistake Mr Biedermann made was his failure to keep insisting on a straight answer. Specifically, he allowed the arsonists to turn him into their buddy and an accomplice to their crime, so that his pride later kept him from publicly admitting his disastrous mistake. This time, things should go a different way. Hence, the first question will be: "What is going on here?" Can the things going on in Facebook groups really be called political discourse? Or are we confusing things here?

The Structure of So-Called Conversations

At first glance, what seems to be going on in the Facebook groups are conversations. But if we look more closely, we find that these "conversations" are different from the conversations and discussions we have in real life or participate in at political party meetings. The first difference is semi-anonymity. Apart from the few scanty variations of emojis, we are not only cut off from non-verbal communication channels in this medium (leading to all the pitfalls and disadvantages we have already encountered with e-mail), we don't even know the true identities of the people using Facebook. All personal information in a user profile can be manipulated at any time; it is no more than a shell covering a nicely draped network node that was electronically generated by the Facebook environment. Hence, we don't know who we are dealing with. Is the user old or young? Is the user serious or just trying to play a role? Is the user an investigative journalist? Or maybe the user is a Russian spy, or the disciple of some Brazilian guru? True, we are right to assume that most people would behave the way we do. They are likely to disclose some of their personal information and be honest with us. But even then we read short texts from total strangers and write them open e-mail messages. How is mutual under-standing possible in such an environment? Isn't it exactly those short statements that are highly dependent on the person uttering them and the context in which they are uttered? On a church congress, the short sentence, "And may God bless you!" has a different meaning than on a leftist party convention. How can any exchange of thoughts work at all in a reduced setting like this?

A social-science experiment that to my knowledge has not been conducted yet could run as follows: Each pupil in a school class is instructed to write messages containing 200 characters each on ten slips of paper and throw them into a big box. Then, at random, the messages are drawn from the box and read out to the pupils without telling them who wrote it. After each message the pupils are asked what they think of it. Will this experiment add to the tensions in the class or relieve them? – The experiment can be conducted with several variations: For instance, the pupils could be instructed to write up the faults of a classmate without mentioning his or her name. In the second round, they could be instructed to guess who wrote a particular sentence and to whom it refers. Of course, the experiment would have to be announced as a game aimed at building mutual understanding and relieving tensions in the class... In the event there had been tensions in the class before the experiment, I venture to guess what the outcome of this test design will be: it will be disastrous for the way the pupils treat one another, causing the situation to spin quickly and totally out of control. Every instant of mistrust, envy, and wounded pride will come to light, and any solidarity there may have been in that class will be damaged beyond repair. Talking about a person without knowing that person is an extremely dangerous communicative situation that is rarely found in real life, yet it is the defining principle of communication via Facebook.

LET US HAVE A LOOK at the way the discussion develops in a Facebook group! As we have seen, the most natural form of communication is face-to-face communication. The people you talk to are in the same place at the same time as you and you have known each other for some time, unless you are Columbus establishing first contact with the natives of the New World. In what way exactly does Facebook abolish this unity of time and place?

Facebook does little to mask its basically technological set-up. Communication is structured like a tree, one that is turned upside down, to be precise. The first posting you can enter, for example the rather trivial question "What are you doing at the moment?", forms the tree's root and remains visible as the "conversation start". Below the conversation start is the comment level, structured like a list. It would be possible to number the comments consecutively, which would allow people to immediately identify the structure as a list. This list proceeds to grow new branches: Item 3 can be expanded by further sub-comments, creating the subordinate items 3.1., 3.2., etc. Even these subordinate items can be commented upon separately, creating a third-level sub-thread (3.1.1. 3.1.2, 3.1.3., etc), though third-level sub-threads get followed rarely.

Facebook's original intention may have been to offer its conversation groups some kind of notice board for publishing opinions and comments. The first user sticks a note stating his opinion to the board and people happening to pass by read the note and stick notes of their own stating their opinions below the first note. On a computer or smartphone screen, however, display options are very limited. With a real-world notice board, there would always be the option to move into the second dimension, arranging the second-level thread horizontally while continuing to arrange the third-level thread vertically. The screen of a computer or smartphone, however, allows only vertical movement: scrolling.

The designers of Facebook were right to assume that very few people's thinking is as structured as theirs. Who would actually be thrilled to plough through a list sub-item by sub-item: 3., 3.1., 3.1.1., 3.2., 3.2.1., 3.2.2.,

46

… Only philosophers like Ludwig Wittgenstein who wrote his *Tractatus logico-philosophicus* in this structured style would enjoy this type of text. Hence, the clever decision was to present the users with only what's absolutely necessary: in addition to the initial posting, users can see only the two or three most recent replies, everything else is hidden from view or packed into an indifferent link saying "View more comments". – Goodbye, lines of reasoning!

Are these message lists an actual conversation? This is hard to imagine because a real-life conversation requires all participants to be in the same place at the same time. Courtesy requires people to answer questions and not ignore anyone completely during the conversation. Facebook has done away with all these rules, for obvious reasons. Yet, Facebook conveys to its users the impression that they are using this medium for reflection and thinking something through together with others in a kind of public brainstorming. – Does Facebook actually work that way?

LET'S OPEN a long Facebook conversation in its entirety to examine it! Anyone attempting to seriously evaluate such "conversations" needs finely tuned philological instincts. As users frequently respond only to the two most recent posts, "conversations" dart this way and that like dialogue in the Theatre of the Absurd: trivial and witty comments, sublime and offensive remarks -

all frequently appear in quick succession, seemingly without any logical connection to one another. This medium is without memory, it keeps bubbling away and seems more like a patient with Alzheimer's who repeats himself over and over.

Yet, among the many branches of this "conversation", we keep stumbling across exchanges that show a coherent thread of conversation. That is because Facebook notifies its users as soon as someone has responded to their posting or comment. When they respond, their reply is integrated into the appropriate branch of the conversation thread. A type of locally open e-mail exchange ensues that may last a couple of hours or days at the most.

As a matter of course, these sudden encounters between strangers as arranged by Facebook - without smiles, handshakes or a joint dinner - do not always take place under a lucky star. As a result, something frequently found at this level of a conversation thread are heated exchanges between opponents who have repeatedly clashed before and simply cannot understand their counterpart's mulishness. Each of them simply wanted to nail their personal opinion to the message board and walk away, but instead they meet someone else wanting to do the same with his - opposing - opinion. Haven't they each made themselves clear enough?

One strong ego locks horns with another equally strong ego in a setting largely unfettered by social conventions. For all intents and purposes, such a situation is almost laughable and more of a funny intermezzo - with a snag though: those involved don't see through the simple set-up of this digital arena and are dead serious about it all. If you take a sober look at the storm fronts clouding this type of Facebook "conversation" you'll find that you're witnessing the emergence of the enraged citizen from the suds of digital small talk.

Users at the top level of the conversation don't get to notice much of these quarrels. Discussions like these ensue as a consequence of Facebook's notification system which links all responses at a sub-commentary level that never makes it to a conversation's top level. If they were to give it some thought, the realisation that they're fighting a lonely fight most of the time would come as a bit of a shock to the squabblers. In general, everybody believing they are showing off to the public - ie a group of about 1,000 members - in an educational discussion is fooling themselves.

WE HAVE TO KEEP CHANGING OUR PERSPECTIVE CONSTANTLY in order to examine how Facebook affects its users! Normal users may not have that much to do with the cockfights going on in the nether regions of sub-commentary. Normal users are sitting in a bus or train and scrolling through their digital inbox, reading only the main level postings that contain video clips and links. The point is not to *understand* opinions and how they relate to the world, the point is to *judge* them as fast as possible: Love ... haha ... wow ... sad ... angry.

Facebook is in vogue and tells us what is "hot". "Hey, just seen that red purse. Think I should get it? „Wow". "300 Euros, though". "Sad!" - That is the strength of Facebook, and probably the main answer to the question what the current purpose of Facebook is. Facebook is a driver of trends - that's its business concept! - that simultaneously conducts market research.

Again: Does this medium encourage political discourse? Can it be used in prudent fashion? The political Facebook groups are more like shopping malls offering opinions. Any user rapidly scrolling through the loosely arranged collection of aphorisms does not behave differently than a consumer strolling down a shopping mall. She evaluates everything she sees, buying one item and ignoring another. But most of the messages run past her without leaving any traces in her memory.

Granted, a Facebook user can also be active and get involved, which is the most tempting offer of all. She can stop at one of the booths and try the eye shadow, lipstick, or rouge, and write a review about them. Let's see what happens! The user has added another twig to the constantly sprouting branches of the multidimensional opinion tree. Granted, the user's report must add a new angle, which is frequently achieved by being more emotional or by placing things in an even more daring context. Facebook acts as a booster simply by the way it was designed. Be brief! Be clear expressing your opinion! Top anything that was said before!

Commenting in itself is an invitation to join in. Post a comment of your own! Are you mulling over something you found somewhere on the Internet? Is the message striking a chord with you? Do you support it? Or categorically reject it? Either way, share it! Write a snappy caption for it! If other people share your opinion, they will tell you. And your chances of being "Liked" are good. You often read comments providing evidence that things are even worse...

The post has been sent. Hungrily, you wait for responses. When are the Likes going to come in? But you will only get Likes if the opinion you have published is shared by the majority in the group. You either adopt that majority opinion or switch to another group.

IS FACEBOOK AN EDUCATIONAL FACILITY? An outlandish thought if you look at all the passive Facebook users scrolling hastily through their daily fill of messages. They are only prime targets for manipulation, because they hardly delve any deeper into the topics Facebook is bombarding them with. That's the opposite of education! Active Facebook users, on the other hand, are concerned with forwarding news and teaching others something. Facebook does switch people into lecturing mode. Are the Facebook conversations then some type of study group? Does that make Facebook a type of self-organised night school for political education? Some active Facebook users might like to think so.

But, as usual, that gut feeling is wrong, and the "Bildungsbürger" (intellectual and economic upper bourgeoisie) enthusiastic about Facebook confuses the new media with the traditional media. - True, anyone posting a message or writing a comment is actively dealing with a subject. They are learning something about it, and, like in school, stand up in front of a group and give a presentation. But who exactly is this "group" that is supposed to play the part of teachers or at least a school class of sorts? What qualifications does this group possess and what is its curriculum? Facebook's method of creating groups is highly abstract with virtually none of the members knowing each other in real life. Groups are formed around a particular topic that their members perceive to be a mutual concern. What exactly is it that you are doing when you keep exposing yourself to judgement from such a faceless mass? Facebook users believe they are making some kind of public impact, but who is this "public"? And, more importantly, what is the price for their public appearance?

THERE IS ONE ESSENTIAL DIFFERENCE between Facebook and its namesake, the book: Facebook was not made for eternity, it does not document anything. Facebook was meant to be a chat; only a prig would store whole years of Facebook message exchanges or conversations. The large mass of Facebook users find this somehow reassuring. Posting your opinion on Facebook does not accidentally land you in a pact with the devil. *Absolvo te!* Facebook groups - as a rule - don't require commitment. No one cares whether you come or go. Once you leave the Facebook group, you are a clean slate again. The group's one thousand members dissolve into thin air, without playing the slightest role in real life. Apart from that, only the company Facebook may know their exact number. I estimate that a post is visible one day per 1,000 group members. After that, it will disappear from the scrollable main window like so much water under the bridge.

#ScrewtheEstablishment!

Mark Zuckerberg may not even have been aware of what he was creating at the time he implemented the simple communication system that more than 1.86 billion people are actively using by now.[2] He understood the term "equal rights", which each democratic state should ideally grant its citizens, to mean "equal node-access rights". He designed human freedom as a possibility for each Facebook user to generate new network nodes and manage their profiles and connectivity by themselves. He also seemed to have an only rather vague concept of the political middle ground without which democracy would not be able to exist: he probably imagined it as some sort of statistical average. So, according to the law of large numbers, opinions would average out, if his Facebook community continued to grow. This would lead to a process of assimilation and stabilise society to the extent the political middle ground got into closer contact with the fringes. Unusual ideas developed by the political fringes would penetrate faster to the political middle ground, undergo critical review there, and get adopted, provided they were good. The evolution of society would get a positive boost.

---

[2] Cf Wikipedia dated March 6, 2017. Counted as active are all users logging on at least once a month.

Is this how society works? In real life, ie the world of conversation as we know it, we know the person voicing his or her opinion and have an idea of their knowledge and experience. We appreciate one another as professionals in particular areas, where our special knowledge gives a different weight to our statements, depending on the topic under discussion. In a discussion about the pros and cons of nuclear power plants, a physicist is more knowledgeable than a layperson; in questions concerning social equity, social workers and the disadvantaged themselves must be heard; in a discussion of religious tolerance, it is specifically the scientists of religion and the scholars of the involved religions who are called upon. This hierarchy of professional expertise is something social networks do not reflect at all so far. Quite the contrary, Facebook is a head-on assault on any form of professional expertise. Every person who has specialist knowledge is subjected to the same treatment: his or her professional expertise simply gets ignored. The Professor of Constitutional Law can write a commentary in an effort to straighten out the misrepresentation of a situation, but an 18-year-old schoolgirl can write his explanation out of sight by simply posting a new message.

STILL, FACEBOOK NURTURES the dangerous misconception that its discussion forums are a digital representation of real-life discussion groups, that the conversations taking place on Facebook are just like normal face-to-face conversations, the only difference being that everybody has the same rights and importance. Facebook users do indeed feel liberated from all forms of hierarchy: at long last they have found a medium where they can indulge themselves and where their opinion gets accepted and heard by the public. Yet, spontaneously, they still abide by the old rules of communication they learned in analogue life. One of these unwritten rules says: The more often an argument is repeated, the more important it is, therefore it bears consideration before other issues. – The reason: the person presenting stronger arguments will be listened to sooner than other conversation participants giving arguments that appear to be weaker.

This law of blending in with the mainstream can be found in all areas of life. Frequently played music must be better than rarely played music. Its popularity alone is proof enough that people are right to appreciate this music. Originality, on the other hand, will develop only through your own actions and thinking. Wherever you show weakness and haven't got the strength to develop your own point of view, you will conform with existing majorities. This conforming to majority can ultimately prompt you to completely deny your own, direct experience, as Solomon Asch impressively demonstrated in his notorious *Asch Conformity Experiments* (1951).

Asch invited the subjects of his experiment to participate in a supposed study about perceptual tasks. Sitting together with a group of other participants they were supposed to compare the length of lines: one line, on the left, was the reference line, three lines on the right could be shorter, longer, or match the length of the reference line. The investigator now instructed the group to say which of the three lines on the right had the same length as the reference line. The person to be tested in the experiment, however, did not know that the other test subjects were really actors who had agreed that they would unanimously give an obviously wrong answer at various occasions. How would the real subject react? The shocking result was that 75 percent of all subjects could be swayed and matched their own response to the majority response even though directly visible evidence showed that the majority response was wrong.

The tendency of humans to conform may be an anthropological constant inherent in all of us. The question is only how society will cope with this fact. Societies have to adapt to constantly changing realities. They cannot afford, in the long run, to walk collectively into Asch's Conformity Trap and close their eyes to reality. Reality is something that needs to be observed with as many eyes and from as many perspectives as possible in order to bring about a reasonable consensus, a congruence in perception (Latin "con" = together, +"sentire" = perceive). Especially the political middle ground is not merely a statistical mean value, it is a cultural achievement that needs to be defined in a constantly ongoing process by any state striving for domestic peace. Until recently, it has been the public media who defined the "political middle ground" by giving "public opinion" a voice. The participants in this public discourse came from many different social groups: political parties, associations, churches, cultural institutions, entrepreneurs, trade unions, etc, and contributed their own, unique perspective to the process of shaping opinions. There is no standardised discourse across all these systems. Each of them defines its own hierarchy, its own way of using language, and its own field of expertise. Their professional experts acted as opinion leaders on television or via other traditional media, because the chance to speak was primarily offered to them. So they shaped public opinion and along with it, the political middle ground.

The traditional media - radio, television, newspapers, etc - used to have a very responsible task they needed to fulfil. Public broadcasters, for example, try to present a balanced cross-section of the various opinions and positions by giving their respective advocates a chance to speak. The purpose of such a cross-section is to present the big picture of the various, existing "originalities". A leftist or rightist newspaper, on the other hand, should use political discourse to analyse existing conditions from their particular point of view and develop their own, original position. In a healthy democracy, there are many different political positions that did not evolve overnight and are based on interaction centred around the political middle ground.

THE SOCIAL MEDIUM FACEBOOK CHALLENGES THIS ENTIRE PROCESS, or more precisely: Facebook ignores it by simply initiating a different process. The basic situation is similar to Asch's Conformity Experiment: in a Facebook group, people find themselves mostly among strangers who all have access to the same possibility of voicing their opinion. In the constant whirl of groups forming and disbanding again there seem to exist sub-systems comparable to traditional associations. Yet, they lack the binding force, the moderation supplied by an objectively defined hierarchy in which opinions are weighed and assessed by peers. Facebook may create a high pressure to conform, but it does so without any real social context. These are the ramifications of Mark Zuckerberg's decision not to design his social network as an initially scientific medium (including peer reviews, etc) but set it up right from the start as a commercial trend medium.

On Facebook, people share a kind of mainstream opinion that is flighty and disorganised in every sense of these words. So far, professional experts are still mostly absent from this medium, and they are right to have little interest in a medium that was designed for pop culture, offering few possibilities for high-level scientific reflection. Facebook is left to schoolchildren by schoolteachers, to students by university professors, and to young people by old people. The absence of real experts, or the system's tendency to prevent people from recognising real experts, plus enforced conformity means that mainstream opinion on Facebook is really no more than the statistical average of a variegated crowd of people. It comes as little surprise that a Facebook group's mainstream opinion frequently stands in contrast to the professional experts' opinion that used to shape public opinion. Everyone fires off impulsive postings until they find a group sharing their view of things.

This sets off a dangerous dynamism: most people find it tremendously gratifying to go against the mainstream and disagree with the public opinion that the traditional media are so busily generating. These people have suddenly started to think for themselves and feel supported and vindicated by their group: the old media's public opinion is the opinion supported by the "Establishment" that remains in power only because it occupies society's most important positions. It's not true that there are good reasons why the old media are so keen on giving professional experts a chance to speak. Oh no! The "Establishment" has hijacked the old media! But the people's voice will be heard in the new media! What's happening in the Facebook groups is perceived as the "true public" which is only being suppressed by the "Establishment" and its old media!

The term "Establishment" is the un-word of the decade: hazy as it is, it can be used to denounce everything that hasn't seen change for a long time. It is not even possible to find fault with this criticism of the Establishment, because it is true that on occasion old structures get outdated and need to be replaced by something new. The really new thing is the darkly loaded meaning that the term has acquired only recently. In the past, individual groups or people were frequently denounced as the Establishment: Old Money, a political old-boys' network, or a way too self-important general theatre director. For the impressionists, academic-art painters were the Establishment. Today, though, the hash tag *#Establishment* is used for "the politicians", "the civil servants", "the high judges", "the churches" - in short, for every professional trained in some kind of education system and supported by a system that does not, day in, day out, make its presence known via three-line ventilations posted on Facebook. If people really wanted to learn about a subject, if, for example, they sat down for an afternoon with the Chief of Police, whom they were criticising excessively, to simulate all the complexities of a police operation, they would likely draw the same conclusions as the Chief of Police, who is the professional expert. They would at least understand that only people with comprehensive knowledge about police work can be in any position to challenge a Chief of Police and provide a second opinion. The layperson needs to listen to professionals from both sides if he or she wants to be a responsible lay judge. But Facebook users no longer think like that. Facebook makes it easy for them to voice their opinion and lash out in a sweeping attack. They feel they own the truth. The Likes they get from the other users are proof of that!

THE PARALLELS TO THE SITUATION IN GERMANY IN THE 1930s ARE SHOCKINGLY FAMILIAR. The demagogic techniques described by Hitler in "Mein Kampf" include simplification and repetition. In order to reach the widest possible audience, political slogans need to be as simple as possible and *engraved* on people's memories through constant repetition. The crucial simplification though, says

Hitler, is to single out and focus on only one enemy - instead of decrying many antagonists - looming large over everything else.

Facebook does nothing to endorse simplifications and repetitions, yet they can be found everywhere on this medium. I wonder why. Because Facebook messages are brief and the only criterion for belonging to a particular group is sharing the opinion professed there. Logically, the one single enemy of all movements that arise from this type of social media are the #ScrewTheEstablishment, and its ruling tools, the #Media (#liarspress, #fakenews, etc).

This is where tragedy starts. While the Facebook community is ranting about the *#Establishment*, their rants are likely to blind them to the elites of real-world community. Of course, there are family clans, privileged by wealth, education and social standing, who will always float on top like fat on a soup, and, on the other side, there is the constantly growing number of people who have barely any chance of social advancement, along with those who are threatened by socio-economic decline. Only recently Didier Eribon has published an impressive description of the fate of these underdogs. But the subtle differences due to family lineage, or more precisely, family history, do not come to light in the social media. Neither professional experts nor any established systems - "the politicians", "the Police", "big business" - should be heedlessly equated with the elite. Rather, the elite is that stratum of society that succeeds at placing their sons and daughters on the upper levels of the mentioned systems. Yet, this is not what people talk about in the social media, instead they rail against any type of professional expertise.

Donald Trump won the primaries because the Republican Party had been dismantling itself for years by agitating against the Establishment. The social media were over-flowing with the Tea Party and hate of Obama. Donald Trump, whose entire personality fits social media like hand in a glove, simply took advantage of that. He could style himself as the new hope for Rust Belt workers and as an honest fighter against the #Establishment - *the Donald* who never saw anything else in his life than other billion-aires and – the Establishment!

Opinion-Forming in the Virtual Society

So far I have described how Facebook conversations unfold to form this tree-like structure which is more like a consecutive list of statements. What about connectivity, the second basic feature of the Facebook structure? It is especially this connectivity that exposes Facebook's artificiality, because contacts can be made with an unprecedented freedom of choice. This is a freedom we do not have in real life, because at school, at university, or a new workplace or nursing home we move to, we always join an organically grown community that we have to get along with. It is especially the encounter with people who do not share our views that shape our character and help us to mature as persons. Frequently, we are as indebted to our enemies as to our friends, because our enemies are instrumental in forming our personality and delivering us from the illusion that our way to understand the world is the only one. Human institutions generate commitment. No one joins or leaves them quickly, because doing one or the other will have a significant impact on one's life.

Not so on Facebook! Its whole design is geared towards making it an entertainment medium. After all, you don't want to sour your precious down time by having to put up with disagreeable people. For years, Facebook featured only the "Like" button, making people who felt they constantly wanted to click a "Dislike" button simply disconnect. For that purpose, they could either remove the offending user from their list of Facebook "friends", or they resigned from the group where they kept running into opposition. A group more to their liking could soon be found. From its inception, Facebook was designed to be a decidedly liberal medium: live and let live. People are free to draw their own lines wherever they wish, or to express themselves freely within the boundaries of lines drawn by others. Anyone who gets excluded ceases to exist, they are literally "out of the picture", and leaving a group is like switching off the TV set: you get silence.

The other users' freedom to exclude someone is not always a pleasant thing to deal with. By their own account, countless schoolchildren have become victims of cyberbullying. They were excluded from entering a group of fellow pupils who stayed in touch among themselves, presumably talking about the excluded pupil. The ostracised pupil had no way of defending her- or himself, because people get included or excluded at the discretion of the group administrator. Facebook provides a platform for archetypal backbiting, something that also happens in the political conversation groups: when a group has formed for the purpose of disparaging and vilifying politicians, the people who might defend them are usually *not* connected to this group. When incorrect information about a person is posted, it takes a long time for someone sympathetic towards the victim to learn about the misinformation. And how are victims supposed to defend themselves? They do not even know into what channels the misinformation went. Facebook is an ideal breeding ground and dissemination platform for prejudice and defamation.

THE BOX IN WHICH PEOPLE LOCK THEMSELVES by invariably choosing the group or friends sharing their views and opinions has recently been criticised as an "opinion-filter bubble" or "echo chamber". Over time, the average Facebook user moves towards a kind of "life in the bubble" in which the discussions he engages in or the news she gets to read will cement and radicalise their original point of view instead of challenging it. The founders of Facebook probably believed that the newest thoughts and ideas would spread in waves, initiating a competition of ideas that would lead to a previously unprecedented diversity of opinions. What they didn't take into account, though, was the intellectual lethargy of the people seeking primarily rest and recreation after work. Like television, which owes its success largely to the fact that people do not have to talk to each other but can surrender themselves to a purely receptive stance without getting overwhelmed by a feeling of loneliness, Facebook is a medium that allows users to remain passive and still enjoy the feeling that they can interact if they want to, that their opinion is called for at all times - if only by clicking on a Like. This stance that users adopt is an affirmative one: they want to go no further in their reflections than they already have and at the same time agree with anybody who shares a similar point of view. This is where Facebook shows that it is an entertainment medium.

Objection! The proverb goes: Birds of a feather flock together. Facebook can't be blamed for the fact that like-minded people connect on this platform. In daily life, too, society orders itself without requiring legislators to impose rules. There are many invisible boundaries assigning people to different groups and thereby creating the diverse society as we know it. What's supposed to be wrong with voluntarily splitting up into different groups? Political parties, too, chosen by the German Basic Law as the bodies responsible for shaping political will, are by their very nature associations of like-minded, or at least similarly-minded people. Facebook does mirror our society, doesn't it?

Extreme caution is required if you do not want to miss the feature that is new in a novelty! The process of shaping political will in a political party or parliament is very different from the process used on Facebook. For shaping political will in the long-standing traditions of democratic countries, people meet at real places like a pub, the meeting room of a local group, or a guildhall specifically rented for the party convention. All attendees bring their faces and personalities to the meeting. In smaller meetings, people know one another well, in large conventions people at least know who the main speakers are. One attendee has links to industry and commerce, another one is a real estate agent, the next one entered politics via a nature conservancy society, yet another one got involved in a citizens' initiative, etc. Interests are an integral part of human life, just look at the word's Latin roots: "interest" = s/he/it takes part); there is no such thing as a person without interests. Consequently, democracy is not defined by refuting interests, it is defined by balancing them. In the old way of shaping political will, interests are not invisible, like on Facebook, they are part of a politically active person's biography which - at least in part - is also known to the public. In the small local groups all members know one another and nobody can rise through the ranks without repeatedly introducing him- or herself to the public. It may be possible to forge a doctoral thesis or to hush up quite a few things, but not everything can be manipulated, and there is always the possibility that the public may find out about a fraud.

INSTEAD OF A POLITICAL PROFILE formed by a person's biography, we now have a Facebook profile which is initially nothing more than an empty, grey oval showing a neck and a head that we can replace by adding a photo of our choice and explain using descriptions of our choice. Political background: unknown. Where a dialogue exchanging arguments between two group members ensues despite this environment, it takes place out of context. You have to be watchful and figure out who you are actually dealing with.

Until previously, politics - the "strong and slow boring of hard boards" as Max Weber put it - took place primarily in the political parties which are also mentioned as constitutional bodies in the German Basic Law. Each party represents a political tradition, has a history and a party manifesto, with its political position expressed in all of these things, presenting a somehow coherent picture. Many people have been discussing these things, making suggestions and discarding them, until they arrived at something one could call a political opinion. Opinions must be formed and then shaped in a process. They are not brainwaves, nor the ability to fire off political witticisms at each and every thing. On the other side of opinion-making were the public media, also embedded in some kind of context through their particular history, local base and political convictions. Their journalists vouched for the quality of their research, and grave mistakes usually had at least some personal consequences for the journalist who made them.

What is it that social media offer in their stead? They simplify and accelerate the opinion-forming process by overriding every single self-regulation mechanism of the old system. At the same time, they distance themselves as far as possible from any type of professional expertise. What respect is there for any of the people contributing to the old opinion-forming process? Is there any politician or journalist adhering to an old-fashioned work ethic when doing his job who does not get inundated with ingratitude and scorn as soon as he opens his Facebook account?

Is there some kind of opinion-forming process taking place at all in the social media? This can be seriously doubted. President Trump acceded to power by using the social media to his advantage, but the world is still guessing as to what his intentions actually are. His political agenda is anything but clear. He is the first President of the United States who obviously waited until he had acceded to office before beginning to shape his political will.

Other political movements arising from social media - I'm thinking of the Arab Spring protest movement or the Brexit advocates - fell apart the moment they had made their breakthrough. It became suddenly clear that the people behind these movements did not feel connected by anything except the hash tag *#Antimubarak* or *#Antieuro*. They did not have a political agenda, and, after all, how could they? How are the social media supposed to produce political thinking that could be called coherent? They were not made for the process of shaping political opinion. In a world in which political statements made by total strangers pile up to form a quickly melting snowball of "dismay rhetoric" it is impossible to map the complexity of politics. Hence, it is a mistake to interpret movements forming in the Facebook environment as a political movement or, worse, a political party. These active members of a Facebook group have no party manifesto and, as a group, would be unable to formulate one. They don't even know each other, so how are they supposed to compare notes and align their political opinions? Facebook only allows them synchronised access to a platform where they can publish their thoughts on one point or other. They will never know whether they developed their beliefs for the same reasons, because their opinions do not get placed within a bigger political context.

Facebook stands for a technocratic view of human interaction and communication. The birds of a feather flocking together in the Facebook model are the mathematical intersection of all network nodes sharing certain common features. The social media do not distinguish between our penchant for a particular cooking recipe or our political likes and dislikes. This unsophisticated model could not be further from being the mirror of a society that is made up of living humans and held together by countless traditions. Consequently, the hash tags under which groups gather are nothing but the rough stitches with which the social media sew up their own versions of Frankenstein's monster.

Anyone knowing which tune to play can make people dance to his tune. Donald Trump knew how to bring around Ku-Klux-Klan members and orthodox Jews, Rust-Belt workers and multi-billionaires alike to support his "movement". What a feat of nihilism!

From Clear-Cut Front Lines to Civil War

The damage Facebook in its current shape is doing to society, "society" including all societies of the world, lies not only in its pretence to be a tool that makes political opinion-shaping more diverse and democratic - which it does not - but also in its speed and feedback effects.

E-mail technology already poses risks, because it allows copying messages infinitely and spreading them around the globe at incredible speed. The social media following in its wake are the serial IT versions of a tsunami washing information into every nook and cranny. At present, the people developing these platforms share only one ideology: "Faster is better." Information that in the past centuries had to take the laborious and long way by road or ship to spread, like the art of papermaking coming from China to Europe, got passed on ever faster. The sailing ship, the steam ship, the transatlantic phone cable: acceleration has always brought advantages. From a developer's point of view, any type of information should be available all over the world within a minute. The Share function to forward postings to all friends (and their friends) serves only this single purpose. Boring information - a description applicable to the most of the available information - will certainly be slowed down, but interesting information will be pervasive: it can spread exponentially.

Thessa's birthday party 2011 gave cause for first doubts concerning this system. The sixteen-year-old schoolgirl accidentally posted a public invitation for her birthday party because she had ticked the wrong box in her account settings and received 5000 accepts the day before the party. Although she sent cancellations, her home was run over by a raucous crowd of 1,600 adolescents who could only be controlled by a large-scale police operation.[3] So far, this incident is an amusing anecdote in recent German history and likely to raise chuckles. But it could be something different altogether. What if a public figure were to rouse hate against minorities among his Facebook friends and Twitter followers and then give the go-ahead by posting or tweeting: "Take up your machetes!"

This information-spreading system capable of mobilising huge crowds by way of a chain reaction leaves society vulnerable to attack. The police can't plant undercover agents in all existing Facebook groups, so mass demonstrations can easily be organised from scratch in groups cultivating such a volatile atmosphere. Weak states - and their number has risen rapidly over the last

---

[3] "Spiegel" online, section „Panorama", June 4, 2011

few years - can easily be pushed to the brink by a concerted attack of this type.

As already mentioned, Facebook is not a medium that encourages reflection, it is a medium that breeds emotional agitation. This is where its built-in potential of high-speed dissemination carries the biggest risk. After a political party meeting, people still have the time to mull everything over on their way home before having the next conversation. This slowness, both in thinking and the dissemination of opinions, is part of the political opinion-forming process and acts as a protective barrier against rash and thoughtless actions and words. Even during the darkest times of German history - which do bear mentioning here - it was not that easy to incite the people. For *years*, Goebbels had been romanticising the "night of the long knives" in the hope that normal citizens would rise in masses against the Jews during the "Reichskristallnacht" (Night of Broken Glass). But they didn't; there was no eruption of the "people's wrath", all that took place was a scheduled operation conducted by NS "goon squads". With a snappy tweet and a few Youtube clips forwarded by NS party members via Facebook to non-party members, Goebbels could have achieved far more, that much can be said even without waxing polemic.

EVERYBODY THINKS THEY KNOW what is happening on Facebook; after all, they have many friends and are members of Facebook groups. Yet, what the masses are really doing while on Facebook is something no one knows for sure - except Mark Zuckerberg, the boss of the closed-circuit show, and possibly a number of intelligence services that wormed their way into all digital back rooms. Facebook has established a kind of semi-public where you can only go as far as open doors will let you. Who really knows how many groups there are? Who knows what the real networks underlying the circles of friends look like?

Let's stay with the question what the effects of Facebook's system of doors and back rooms are. What are the ramifications of this globally accessible digital open-plan office in which everybody can shift the partitions walls any way they want? - As I've said already, the initial hope that the system would lead to a steady propagation of opinions and fair discussion of the differing approaches turned out to be an illusion. On Facebook, information does not steadily diffuse like gas filling a room, it flows out, forming swirls and eddies that may spin around in the same place for a long time. In theses swirls and eddies (I consider this analogy taken from fluid physics more fitting than the image of the bubble) the users endorse each other's opinions, and those begging to differ soon withdraw to another eddy or swirl. Based on the keywords that Facebook finds in their postings, users even get fully automated suggestions which groups they might like best. Unless they are headed for confrontation with their groups or friends, users will be left in peace. Their surfing habits will easily carry them from group to group until they find the swirl they like best. Once a user has found "his" swirl, he will be buoyed and supported by it, a driver while being driven at the same time, and find pleasant entertainment in this titillating environment. Nothing would make him think that his seemingly innocuous behaviour could throw society as a whole off-balance. That is because he does not get to see "society" itself, but only that section of society he is currently connecting with. The only person to see the Facebook community in its entirety - with "community" referring to all eddies and swirls, or more precisely, the full number of network nodes, their connections and messages - is Mark Zuckerberg, the entrepreneur. It's bizarre how he used a couple of PHP programs to create a virtual society that functions along totally different lines than real-life society! Zuckerberg's network is a bustling forum of arbitrariness. Make no surmises concerning real-life society! Everything here is interconnected, gets repeated over and over again, is an agitator or an honest idiot: but what can be considered to be representative? All methods of opinion-polling established over the last few decades are totally useless on Facebook. People feel like they are all *in*, while they really maybe totally *out*.

RADICALISATION GETS FREQUENTLY mentioned in connection with social media. It is said that today's radicals are more intelligent than those of the past, because they make use of social media which enable them to set up loosely structured organisations that are difficult to break up. This is not even half the truth. - Sure, the radicals have decided to use this new technology; but the process itself works in the opposite direction: it is Facebook use that leads to radicalisation.

Imagine a young man struggling with more difficulties in life than others because he can't seem to cope with the German education and work systems. There may be many different reasons for his problems: maybe he is from a family less inclined to education, or a family of immigrants with language difficulties, or maybe his intellectual abilities are simply below average. If this person with special needs is denied the appropriate additional support at school, his life will be nothing but frustrating: he will always be the nitwit whose voice doesn't count and who everybody seems to find fault with. Suddenly, he discovers Facebook and finds a group somewhere in which other people share his points of view. For the first time, his ego gets a boost rather than a blow. He is overwhelmed by people's kindness. They feel exactly the same way as he does! But soul snatchers of every colour are already hard at work in that group, let's take islamists, just by way of example. "You're a valuable person, too!" "They only wanted to put you down!" "It wasn't your fault. It was Allah's doing, so you would come to him." What a revelation!

In Facebook's entire structure the possibility of radicalisation is a built-in feature, it is actually the most natural course of "education" for anyone completely immersing him- or herself in this medium. The tone of Facebook messages is emotional and little suited to the exploration of rational arguments and counter-arguments; the spectrum of opinions in these groups is narrow, and algorithms always make fully automated suggestions for yet another, more radical group. There are virtually no impediments to joining such groups, because there don't seem to be any risks involved. As a result, the diversity of people one gets into touch with diminishes more and more. At the same time, Facebook's privacy settings make it easier for people to block "friends" that don't share their views, which leads to a gradual, self-imposed isolation. And people go into self-isolation genuinely believing themselves to be particularly critical minds! Agitators, on the other hand, have the entire arsenal of manipulation tools at their disposal - without any risks involved *because of* Facebook's privacy policy. If they don't happen to be the head of al-Qaeda, of all people, anybody can join the fray under any identity they like. They can fabricate conversations by running several Facebook accounts simultaneously, create and forward fake news, and last but not least, they can hermetically seal their group off to any intrusion from outside. And the whole thing works on a global scale: You wouldn't stay alone even if only 0.001% of all people supported your point of view. - Where in the world can you find a setting or environment more amenable to propagating radicalism?

FACEBOOK BRINGS TOGETHER WHAT DOES NOT BELONG TOGETHER. It is already connecting the entire world: the company Facebooks connects people from different cultural backgrounds with one another, and it does so without bothering to give cultural differences any thought. The misapprehension that the meaning of a three-line statement should be non-contextual leads to excesses of the worst kind. It really takes a full course of university studies of learning about a foreign culture before one can even begin to understand it. What lies at its core, what is only outward appearances? Without any sense of context it is impossible to interpret this plethora of information. This is why the traditional media, and also businesses, are happy to take advice from specialists when they wish to enter into relations with foreign states; but on the Internet, and especially in the social media, everybody is living in a world of his or her own. The little notes these people read are placed in the readily available context of their own personal worlds.

They don't even make an effort to explore the context in which the information is provided. An error with calamitous consequences: people filter out the statements they perceive as typical of the other side and use them to build and expand on their own bias/prejudices.

We certainly didn't behave like this in the past with the old media, namely television and newspapers! Looking back, most of us used to be a relatively loyal audience sticking to only the same few newspapers or TV news channels. As a result, we would receive information and news that the heads of department had reviewed in editorial meetings. We would watch the whole programme and read the whole newspaper, getting confronted in the process with issues that did not appeal to our emotions. So, before we even started to privately categorise the facts of an event or situation we had already received a lot of information concerning its context. We had learned to look at the big picture, we didn't piece together little sticky notes to compose an arbitrary collage of opinions.

But on Facebook, things are even worse: for any "pro-something" group, there is also an "anti-something"-group. There are islamistic groups and anti-Islam groups; pro-establishment groups and anti-establishment groups; groups with Irish Catholics and groups with Irish protestants; in Syria, every militia doubtless runs a Facebook group of its own. Members of a group working each other up lose their ability for true exchange with people from other swirls and eddies. Fatally enough, such opposing groups still share enough points of contact for information to flow to and fro. The al-Qaeda supporter wishing to pour fuel into the fire only needs to look around in the groups supporting Geert Wilders or Thilo Sarrazin in order to lay hand on abundant proof that the West is planning the destruction of Islam. Conversely, on the web sites of radical muslims, right-wing populists can find plenty of Quran quotes that are suggestive of imminent doom. On this roller coaster of extremism, any form of reason loses out. Those on the inside no longer want to hear the voices of moderation and accuse them of glossing things over or even of "treason". Even discerning, highly-educated people cave in on Facebook, without realising it, and allow themselves to be drawn into a one-sided view of information. Among Facebook users, for example, the only accepted expert on Islam is Hamed Abdel-Samad whose audacious historicisation and even psychologisation of the Prophet obviously strikes a chord with his audience. The many other good descriptions of Islam written by prominent experts and available in book shops everywhere simply get ignored. Woe to those who won't go to a book shop before they turn to Facebook for information!

Nobody should expect the social media to provide a cure for their problems! I am not aware of a single instance of someone coming to terms with his problems thanks to social media! Wherever are there two opposing groups that sat down together to actually talk? I only hear of escalations and the resurgence of old conflicts. - Or did the rift between the white and the African-American population in the US become any smaller in the era of Facebook? Now here's something that warrants investigation. Like the question whether the peace process in Colombia will continue if Mark Zuckerberg succeeds with his "Free internet for Colombia" initiative launched in 2015. When, finally, all FARC rebels down to the last village are connected via Facebook and those voting "no" in the peace referendum exchange posts about their feelings of justice, an era of harmony will dawn for the country!

Facebook is a trend medium. It lives off trends and has been optimised for generating trends. The faster Facebook can categorise people, the more effective its advertising to them can be. Which is why the formation of different strata lies in a media company's interests. If a majority of senior citizens loves black spectacle frames and the majority of young people loves red ones, Facebook will support each group in their preference. Once a trend has been established, it will make Facebook's tills ring. It's not much of a surprise that Facebook drives political polarisation, or is it? That algorithms test the ground by suggesting one radical group after another to users? This is a blatantly mindless process, because the technicians didn't think it necessary to teach their algo-rithms the difference between politics and toothpaste.

Twitter - Leading Opinion Through Self-Advertising

"What? You seek something? You wish to multiply yourself tenfold, a hundredfold? You seek followers? Seek zeros!"
(Friedrich Nietzsche)

The sound of a small bird twittering and warbling to attract the attention of a female has undoubtedly inspired the name and logo of Twitter, the second large social medium. Launched in 2006, Twitter initially styled itself as a type of personal diary that users could make available to a broad public via SMS. It seemed like a very outlandish offer to make: who would want their personal diary to be publicly available in a library that's accessible to the whole world, of all things? But Twitter was correct in its assessment of human vanity and people's tendency towards exhibitionism. The diary column's limited space led to Twitter's famous rule that a "Tweet" is restricted to 140 characters.

Normal users might take it easy, treating their accounts like the good old leather-bound note book. They might tweet diary entries like that written by Thomas Mann: *"I am frequently feeling so unwell, especially on the days I shake my bowels"* (June 25, 1955), and nobody would take umbrage. At best, a couple of life insurance companies and suppliers of colon care products would be his followers. If all inhabitants of a small town were to store their diaries on a shelf in the local public library, it will be highly unlikely that someone would pick my personal diary from the shelf. Only people I also know in real life - friends, but also enemies - would pick it up occasionally. Apart from that, the only person to pick it up regularly would be the librarian - in order to dust it. It's the same with Twitter: normal users have few followers and amuse primarily themselves by tweeting.

At first, a user searches for hash tags that he himself wishes to follow. He can tell his real-life friends that he is now on Twitter too, and, thrilled at having found another person there, they can subscribe to each other as followers. Despite this, there is no denying the fact that private individuals are usually hard-put to attract followers. It is easy to find guidance on the Internet as to how a company can quickly recruit a base of followers to promote its business. But this is hardly a viable option for users who are interested in politics and seeking partners for discussion. So they won't bother to. It is impossible to frame a reasonable thought in just 140 characters anyway. So what!

Now what is it that makes Twitter interesting as a political medium after all? – If the social media were parts of a house, e-mail would be the foundation, Facebook the walls, and Twitter the roof. You could also say, Twitter plays the tune to which Facebook dances. Twitter does away with the façade of equality that Facebook still manages to keep up somehow. Facebook enables users to join groups the day they sign up and start discussions in front of thousands of people. Twitter, on the other hand, is clearly more hierarchical in structure: some users have a million followers while others have none. Some people are major players, others simply consumers.

WHAT IS IT THAT MOVES PEOPLE to take part in this uneven play of forces after all? It is, again, the vague nature of the social media that comes to bear here. What do you use them for, what is their purpose? The idea of Twitter being a diary was definitely outdated in record time. Today, Twitter is called an "online news service", a term that leads to severe misunderstanding by suggesting, albeit correctly, that news can be distributed via Twitter. Because Twitter is effective only in conjunction with other media, it is really a type of parasite. You can attach a home-made YouTube video clip to your tweet, an URL, or a link to a particularly interesting programme that you recommend in your tweet. The 140-character main message provides merely a superficial categorisation, like some type of label. The pivotal element is the attachment.

Let's get back to Mr Biedermann! Because it is the latest rage, he has signed up with Twitter and found that his tweets don't really matter. Still, he decides to take advantage of the "online news service". He subscribes as a follower to the TV stations ARD, ZDF, the daily newspaper Frankfurter Allgemeine Zeitung, and two political parties he deems eligible for election. Effective immediately, these institutions send him their tweets, ie their personal diaries. ARD and ZDF send an attachment with an overview of the daily news, the Frankfurter Allgemeine Zeitung sends Mr Biedermann an article from its online edition free of charge. "Now that's convenient," thinks Mr Biedermann, "I'll be able to stay on top of current affairs even when I don't get to buy the newspaper at the stall." Twitter hasn't changed a thing for him. On the contrary, his quality of life has improved again.

Mr Biedermann behaves correctly - in a way: he entrusts the selection of the news he gets to see on Twitter to the media he has long been accustomed to. If Mr Biedermann were to subscribe as a follower to thousands of people, it would be impossible to display the profusion of messages rushing into his account on the screen. And what is the solution the technicians have found to solve the display problem? - An algorithm, of course, to bring order to the chaos. Even when searching for keywords like *#merkel* or *#associationlaw*, an algorithm using obscure criteria decides which tweet appears at the top.

If Mr Biedermann continues to be wary, doesn't subscribe to too many people, and doesn't too frequently conduct his own searches for hash tags, he will never know that he has already given up control of something essential: his prerogative to decide for himself which source of information he chooses and what information he deems important or unimportant. "Wait, wait," chirps a voice from the sidelines, "Mr Biedermann selected the media he follows on Twitter with deliberation by choosing the Frankfurter Allgemeine Zeitung over the *Süddeutsche Zeitung*. He is free to change his mind any time, that means he'll keep his full autonomy in this respect!" - Granted, but the articles sent by the Frankfurter Allgemeine Zeitung are only a small part of the whole newspaper. How do these small parts get selected? The Frankfurter Allgemeine Zeitung is probably interested in sending a particularly interesting article, thereby making sure that readers actually buy the printed newspaper at the next occasion. But is the article they sent really the most interesting one? Since they realised that they are getting strong competition from social media, the traditional media have signed up with the social media and are now unable to get away from emotional issues. The carefully redacted print edition of the Frankfurter Allgemeine Zeitung and the Twitter news feed compiled by an algorithm are two totally different things.

IN REALITY, TWITTER is an online *news screening service*, not an online news service. Depending on the way it is used, this service can change its appearance completely. Mr Biedermann perceives it as a type of promotional flyer for the reputable media he usually turns to for information. To understand what exactly normal users get out of Twitter, one has to look at its creators. In the big news orchestra conducted by Twitter, the traditional media are just one group of instruments, and not even the most important one at that.

Although "Twitter has yet to earn money from its operations"[4] (in other words: it is still living off company shares and expectations for the future), the parties particularly interested in it are businesses seeking to boost their sales. No brand can have a bigger dream than collecting as many followers as possible on Twitter: that way you get promotion at no cost at all. That may be the reason why Donald Trump signed up with Twitter in 2009 in the first place: he wanted to promote his business conglomerate. An ideal basis for taking off on Twitter was Donald Trump's celebrity status which he had earned in previous decades as a playboy and big shot of New York's High Society. To this day, Twitter advises newbies to get their initial bearings by connecting to local celebs, if they don't know whom they should follow; and who would deny that Donald Trump, this billionaire with crazy views, has a high entertainment value? In a sense, Donald Trump was extremely successful: he could advertise his own companies, and, provided he stayed interesting, he was even the crowd-puller of his own promotion. His tastes, his style of living, his excesses made him a brand of US pop culture. But what is it that made this resourceful self-marketeer turn to politics? How could a spark from the shallow world of pop culture fly as far as to the serious field of politics? Here, too, the key word is egalitarianism. On Twitter, pop

---

[4] Frankfurter Allgemeine Zeitung: *„Lohnt sich Twitter noch"* (27.10.2016)

stars and politicians have to stand in the same line as other people. Technically, they're the same type of user.

Those users with millions of followers behind them have the privilege of sending regular tweets to this huge group of people. Even Obama, during his own presidential race, kept in touch with his campaigning team via Twitter, he could send promotional clips and government news to his followers who would share them via Facebook with their groups and circles of friends. Twitter plays the tune, and Facebook dances to it... Obama's presidential race still was a mostly normal election campaign - though boosted by a turbocharger.

Years went by, Twitter and Facebook achieved an ever wider spread and began to be perceived as extensions of the traditional media. That's the point at which Twitter's screening mechanisms came to bear in full force. Anyone with money had already an advantage with the traditional media because their money could buy the media. In Italy, Berlusconi stayed in power solely because he owned TV stations. For Trump and anybody else following in his steps the media costs will be much lower. Basically, all you need is one TV station and one professionally made online newspaper to produce all the news headlines that you recommend in your tweets. Actually, you don't even need these media either, because you can influence the opinion-forming process of millions of people by tweeting your followers the news headlines that you have selected for them.

WHERE TRADITIONAL MEDIA are combined with the news screening medium Twitter you create disastrous synergies. Merely by existing does Twitter place enormous pressure on the traditional media. Once a Twitter user has follower base of a million people, that means, simply put, he has enormous advertising power. A traditional medium has to spend a lot of money in order to reach a million people, while the makers & shakers using Twitter get that kind of reach for free. This is the reason why TV stations, in their reports, cannot afford to ignore individuals possessing such a high multiplier effect. So every TV station will of course include reports about the most prominent Twitter celebrities, hoping that the celebrities recommend the station's report in their tweets: "You scratch my back, I'll scratch yours." By this mutual back-scratching, though, TV stations promote the owners of the respective Twitter accounts, giving them even more power.

There are two lessons to be learned from that: firstly, the social media hold a better strategic position, with the traditional media acting as the anvil to the social media's hammer. Secondly, there is a new gauge for non-egalitarian interaction, namely the number of followers on Twitter. It is not professional expertise and insight that determines a person's influence on public opinion, but the position of power gained over years through a Twitter account. How this concentration of power began to develop is irrelevant: whether it was someone figuring prominently in the German Carnival scene or a foul-mouthed football player who made names for themselves, or the boss of a large company who simply paid his followers money. Each of them can henceforth fire off tweets on any topic as if they were universal experts for everything.

What is truth, Mr Pilatus?

If the social media are a large-scale social-science experiment, Donald Trump is its first prominent result. It is still too early to evaluate his policy. So far, there is no proof that he will go down in history as a bad president. When asked during a presidential debate to name a positive trait of his rival Hilary Clinton, Trump replied approvingly: "She's a fighter." And he honestly meant it - that's how he also sees himself and that's how he acts. Trump's policy will pulverise many things that have been crumbling for a long time. He doesn't even make an effort to understand complicated issues. His approach is not to untie the Gordian knot, but to cut it.

An event that became historic already is the TV appearance of Kellyanne Conway, Counselor to the President, on February 22, 2017. Trump had claimed that the audience witnessing his inauguration had been the largest ever seen at such a ceremony, and White House Press Secretary Sean Spicer had come to his boss's aid. In response, the media gleefully presented pictures of Obama's inauguration, proving that his inauguration had drawn a much larger crowd than Trump's inauguration. During an interview, Kellyanne Conway found herself in the awkward position of having to defend the obviously false statements made by both the White House

Press Secretary and her senior boss. Driven into a corner by NBC reporter Chuck Todd, she said: "Don't be so overly dramatic about it, Chuck! What - You're saying it's a falsehood. And they're giving Sean Spicer, our press secretary, gave alternative facts to that".

Although Trump opponents called them lies in their reactive tweets, alternative facts are not exactly lies, but a *contradictio in adiecto*. There's something wrong here. There is never an alternative to facts: they're either clear or unknown. But in the world through which Conway has been moving these past months - an election campaign run through the social media - her choice of words does make sense. Even among the traditional media, each used to present news with a slightly different take on the facts, the verification process was slow, with the truth lying somewhere in the middle. The social media have raised the number of people who are capable of contributing bits and pieces of information, speeding up the whole process to a point where the verification of facts lags hopelessly behind. This changes the approach to handling facts. Facts are no longer something that is verifiable and whose denial (too rarely) leads to eventual retribution, facts are what a sufficiently large number of people *in the real world* believes to be facts.

Factum in Latin means 'that which was made". In the social media, each swirl and eddy generates its own "facts", and each major player can plant "facts" via Twitter. Makes you rub your eyes in amazement! Did this term really exist before 2010? When the former Europeans introduced the term *factum* into the German or English language, they no longer associated it with the deeds of emperor Augustus. By *factum* they now meant "that which was made by God". It wasn't until the advent of social media that Man started to create facts faster than God could falsify them. – *Veni creator spiritus...*

If we're honest, we have been familiar with this kind of sham for a long time. For decades, we have been tolerating advertisements that brush up reality: "The best chocolate you ever tasted." - "Pritt - the stickiest glue available." - "For us, it's the customer who counts". - No one has ever bothered to verify these claims. We are used to continually hearing them and would never protest because they are untrue. That's the nature of advertising. By design, it includes packaging on which the manufacturer promotes his product; the claims made there are somehow part of the manufacturer's design scope. "Alternative facts" can be found everywhere in promotion. If a manufacturer were to be honest and print what he truly knows about a product on its packaging, he'd risk losing his sales. His colleagues would grin slyly and snicker at his lousy marketing move. In the Bible, prophet Amos raged against such methods, and

Kant, too, was known to repudiate lies at all times. Advertising professionals will defend themselves by claiming that people apparently want to be lied to. After all, they buy products that were openly promoted with lies and deception. The objective of advertising is successful sales, and let's be honest: aren't the people living in the times of capitalism, with its sophisticated advertising methods, far better off than the people living in past centuries, who had a stronger sense of ethics? Truth has to be fast, only then will it be profitable! That is the reason why Kellyanne Conway was honestly surprised at the reporter's insistent questioning. "Don't be so overly dramatic about it, Chuck. It's alternative facts."

ASSUMING WE ACCEPT this new concept of truth and define truth as something that a majority of people *in the real world* believe to be true. What is the difference between the old and the new process of establishing the truth?

An interesting definition of truth says: Truth is what will stand up in a court of law. Scientific research results are indeed accepted only when they pass examination by an expert committee. A newly discovered physical particle will be accepted by science only after it has been presented and discussed at science congresses and, where necessary, confirmed by successful duplication of the experiment. Processes to establish the truth are always slow going and need a particular social structure. Not everybody will make a good judge. – Something similar can be said of the political decision-making process. It is never completely isolated from some kind of social structure, and even in the broad range between authoritarian and liberal social structures, democratic decision-making does not involve everybody to equal parts in the decision-making process. Be it within the family, in a company, or at universities: perfect equality is not possible anywhere.

As I have mentioned already, Facebook assumes that its nodes are egalitarian. At best, the founder, ie the administrator, of a group, can remove users from a group, and has only few other special rights. Apart from that there is no weighting of the voices. A ranking within a group as we know it from daily life does not exist at all. Users are living their lives in a collective where they are less accountable, easier to scare, and have a restricted view of the world.

In contrast, Twitter is not a leveller, it is a game of monopoly written in Ruby programming language and seeking to attain power over public opinion. And since it is based on advertising, Twitter bears no relation whatsoever to the way real-life society is structured. Anybody is welcome to hunt for followers, and, in the manner of the Wild West, the hunting methods are not subject to any rules at all. Julius Caesar used to purchase votes in front of the Capitol; today, purchasing votes is a bit more circuitous. Donald Trump chose the path of the wealthy TV entertainer; Beppe Grillo (current following: 2.3 million) went along the same path with a lot of humour but without the wealth, because he hadn't inherited any. Others use guile: the late Margot Honecker, deceased in 2016, is still twittering on Facebook. That's a witty and revealing move, unmasking the system behind it. The first tweets from this account were sent while the real Margot Honecker was still alive, by the way. But who cares about identity theft in this medium! If someone tricks thousands of fans into following him and achieves undeserved media attention through his trickery - so what!

Quid est veritas? What is truth? A question that Pilatus once asked, shrugging his shoulders.

Humans and the Vision of Humanity in the Social Media

What type of politician are the social media going to breed? What person is so serene that they will be able to put up with the verbal Voodoo exercised by thousands of people behind his back in all those Facebook groups? Would any customer with normal sensitivities like to enter a bakery with the feeling that the shop assistant may have posted hate comments against him only half an hour ago? Only a couple of years ago, if politicians were seen on the street, people used to greet them, sometimes with a smile, even though they might disagree with their policy. What will happen nowadays? Do we really live in rough times, Mr Gauck, former President of the Federal Republic of Germany?[5]

The politicians of the future will have to be narcissists with a big ego. They will need to be impervious to the hate poured out over them. What concern of theirs are alternative truths? They're only spreading a bad smell. You have to represent your brand, you have to unconditionally believe in it and make others believe in it: My perfume will envelop you in the fragrance of a spring meadow in the morning! Feel beautiful and loved with my perfume! If you

---

[5] Cf Joachim Gauck's Parting Speech, cf above.

buy into my truth, you'll be a *winner*, everybody else will be a *loser*, let them rant and rave all they like!

Politicians of the future shouldn't spend too much time pondering over things. No point in keeping the people's long-term interest in sight. Rather, politicians will need to engineer opinions and analyse how to collect a lot of *Likes* in the short run. What's the mechanism behind a pop song hitting the charts via Twitter and Facebook within two weeks, and how can that advertising method be applied for maximum impact in an election campaign? Hitler copied the drama of his staged political rallies from Richard Wagner, and Hollywood continued to uphold this staging tradition for a long time. The politicians of the future will copy their election campaign strategy from Psy and his smash hit *Gangnam Style*.

In terms of its vision of humanity, the fascism seen in Europe in the 1930s is merely the family's ugly old great-aunt in relation to today's policy-making via social-media. For too long, fascism may have been interpreted as a nostalgic aberration and relapse into irrational barbarism, while its alarmingly modern view of the world escaped notice. This failure to notice has come back to haunt us today, giving rise to an unexpectedly fast return of nationalism and defamation politics.

The fans of present-day hash tag movements are obviously not grim *lictors* protecting their *caesar* with their *fasces* (bundle of wooden rods) and axes. Hence, the term "fascism" is misleading, because it suggests the application of violence coming from the top of a state. But in the social media, it is the bottom that applies violence; a state of *followers* doesn't need a caesar, it only needs an efficient marketing strategy. Generally speaking, a state of followers is an ochlocracy ("mob rule") and its leaders dance along with the anonymous crowd, driven by public opinion rather than shaping it. The grisly feature that the new and the seemingly outdated have in common, though, is their contempt of individual human beings whose entire existence gets reduced to just a couple of parameters: "we", "they", "this crazy left-wing fascist" - that's the kind of noise blaring from all corners of Facebook. Each of the speakers believes himself to be at the centre of a world ruled by some anonymous *common sense*.

SOCIAL MEDIA are as good or bad as their users. But since social media don't set up any rules, everybody can turn them to unfair use, if they really want to. When people can push each other out of the way, when crude claims have more effect than informed arguments, when harsh, generalising language presses to the fore and manipulative tricks are suddenly a resounding success, it's the honest people who lose out. Against this backdrop, what's the point of all that academic education, the world of the intellect that over centuries has shaped our current ideal of humanity? Where's the point in rule of law, religion, philosophy, this world's many and rich cultures? Let's quickly hold that up for ridicule! The world has always been one big Facebook! It is all about asserting oneself, no more and no less. Everything is no more than a fight for resources and greed for power! Or is it?

This concept turns any reference to Herbert Spencer, who already advocated white supremacy more than a hundred years ago, into nothing more than a footnote. Spencer considered the Anglo-Saxon nobleman as the apex of evolution, because he was sophisticated, ruled the world through his capital investments and succeeded in asserting himself over his fellow men. These are the exact same reasons why Donald Trump believes in the excellence of his genes.

Donald Trump is not alone with his social-Darwinist concept of humanity. By believing in the total reproducibility of humans through algorithms, the technicians of Silicon Valley are nurturing this idea, too. They pitch their reconstructed humans against each other in computer simulations and - lo and behold: - the matchstick figure with the best parameters always prevails.[6]

The creators of the social media must have been very confident of their assessment of human nature at the time they brought their rustic communication system to the world. They believed that each of us is an average consumer who can be described easily with a couple of variables. As a result, so they believe, it is easy to predict which way the game on the server will go. After all, technology is

---

[6] Frank Schirrmacher (2013), O' Neil (2016)

hard science, and society is an *easy* thing. It will somehow organise itself. Far from it!

The human being is *the* transcendent being. What I am trying to say with this is that whenever one believes to have found the answer to the question "What is the nature of human beings ?", humans will break the pattern. Human beings outpace any theory about human nature for a simple reason: self-reflexiveness doesn't exist; no human being is capable of developing a completely objective view of him- or herself. Even though, based on a brilliant algorithm using all conceivable variables, I might have succeeded at predicting that I would drink tea the next morning, this prediction could be just the reason I went to choose coffee the next morning. It's likely that we humans deliberately change our minds to escape from any form of limitation. Economists believing they can predict upcoming developments by applying lots of science undermine the significance of their prediction just by making it. There will always be those betting on a prediction and those betting against it for good measure. Both sides have already assumed a meta-position, meaning they are detached from the supposed rationality of the presented argument. - Isn't it an irony of world-historic proportions that unpredictability began to reach record highs in exactly the moment when humanity imagined they could predict anything using algorithms?

THE THINKING IN SILICON VALLEY, is predominantly technocratic and joined by an ahistorical mindset. An ahistorically thinking person believes that the language he currently uses and describes his world with can *in principle* be extended to cover all dimensions of time and space. He believes himself in the possession of a language into which all of humanity's thinking can be translated without anything getting lost in translation. To him, language is independent of culture and history.

I imagine a young person who has rapidly climbed the career ladder and is sitting in his car, driving to his workplace located in a drab office building. He is lost in thought, pondering a question going through his mind: What does happiness mean? - "Happiness means freedom. And freedom means that I can afford a nice car. That I've got the time to go on a nice holiday with my family. And that's basically what all people want." That's it! Cheerfully, he approaches his marketing manager: „Hi, Fred! Listen, I've got this idea. Why don't we jazz up our marketing campaign by building it around freedom?" „Cool idea. But what do you mean by freedom?" replies his marketing manager. The young man stops short. Should he tell his marketing manager right away? Cautiously, he makes a suggestion: "Let's make an empirical survey!" - A couple of weeks later, pale students with questionnaires appear on market places all over Germany. Their "field research" objective is to find out whether freedom and prosperity are related in the way people think. And in fact, the result is that people correlate the term freedom with prosperity, the right to vote, good health, owning a house, etc. When all the factors mentioned above come together, the brain presumably produces the reward hormone dopamine, and exactly this process is what we call freedom...

Wait a moment! They say the term freedom is "correlated" with other terms? What is the justification of this assumption? Isn't the question about freedom, asked in quite specific form, based on the assumption that only one quantifiable answer will be meaningful? Couldn't some person have existed at some time somewhere in the world whose understanding of the concept of freedom was essentially different? A concept so different that the parameters employed in the survey do not play any role at all? Only a few pages up I have given you an example of how the concept of freedom could be understood as well. And more, totally different concepts of freedom could exist throughout the world. There even could be foreign cultures who have never in their long-standing history had a word like "freedom", although we wouldn't perceive them as not free if we were to visit them. - In terms of the research objective, these aspects remain entirely out of scope; they are not in tune with that young person's way of thinking, whose inquisitive earnestness sinks him ever deeper into his one-sided view of the world.

Technocracy today bears strange fruit. One has to be blind, dumb, and deaf to miss its basically ahistorical nature. Technocrats are seriously searching for a final storage location in which radioactive waste can be stored safely for 250,000 years. There isn't a single country on this planet that has been able to provide peace and social security for just 250 years! No one would like to imagine what would happen if, say, the IS found a nuclear final storage on their territory. But technocrats think nothing will happen if they only shield a storage zone in a seismically safe region and keep the storage zone's temperature and pressure stable. Something that works for two days will *in principle* work for 250,000 years as well. The technocrat's timeline is the one you find in physics textbooks: it is a succession of egalitarian nodes in time. This timeline doesn't include anything like the IS.

Egalitarian nodes: now where have we heard that before? Yep, social networks. They define all users as egalitarian network nodes: they have no fixed name, no history, no culture - they can try on any role and connect with anybody. - That's exactly the hidden spot where the pullover has a loose thread, so to speak. All one has to do is pull the thread and society comes apart at the seams – along with it everything that has still been standing firm.

HAS IT BECOME CLEAR, AT LAST, that this way of thinking has reached its tipping point, that "calamity" has struck already? We could go on playing the technocratic game and pretend that everything is under control: that Man is an ahistorical creature, that his variables could be empirically calculated down to the last decimal place, that all of humanity's thoughts can be translated irrespective of their cultural background, that everything is headed towards a nameless, homogeneous mass, that we might not be able to communicate well via social media yet, but we would learn with time. The expectation is that a single, common language would establish itself in the social media, namely the present-day language of the technicians who created these media. That is when history would end, all people would think "rationally" and be happy. Yes, we could go on like this.

But what would really happen? At this instant, there's already a Babylonian jumble of languages all over the social media, and it's especially science that gets affected by that. In the future, all sorts of creationist groups will disseminate their videos, using the crudest of arguments to deny the existence of evolution. On Facebook, the groups with users feeling nothing but contempt for scientists will grow ever larger. *This established science community! There are hundreds of arguments available on highly frequented YouTube channels that deny evolution! Goodbye,* science!

By the way, creationism, or religious fundamentalism in general, originates from religious splinter groups and anti-establishment churches, not from the centre of the mainstream religions whose long-standing theological traditions have been reflecting on modernity for quite some time. Religion as exercised by fundamentalists: Mondays: conversion; Tuesdays: Bible-reading; Wednesdays: demonstration for the true Belief in Creation... Like the technocrats, religious fundamentalists subscribe to a binary concept of truth (TRUE or FALSE), and their way of thinking is also ahistorical ("there is no evolution in theological thought, only one absolute truth, valid

111

for all eternity"). This is why fundamentalists and technocrats get along perfectly, and, after all, many fundamentalists have graduated from technical universities. We certainly don't have to worry about the future of religious fundamentalism, given the current state of the social media.

The first place among the long-standing and developing systems that are going toxic under the influence of social media and turning against science belongs to industry and commerce, not religion, which in a way is only a victim. Industry and commerce have long ago made a pact with the technocrats, daily increasing their influence on what science will research and what will be considered scientific truth. The existence of a guiding medium organised along social-Darwinism lines bothers industry and commerce the least, because they have the most ample means to influence that medium.

THE TECHNOCRATIC WAY OF THINKING that seeks to keep all things historical from entering into its conception of the world is reaching its absolute limits and beginning to destroy its own foundations. Max Scheler is finally proven right in his assessment made 1927 that humanity has a spiritual side which is totally different from all types of technological intelligence. During his time, the theory of evolution was already a scientific fact, but Scheler was aware that the traditional reference to human beings as heard in social contexts everywhere cannot simply be equated with the reference to human beings as one of nature's creations. Scheler, for example, quoted the strong

Western tradition that sets God as the point of reference and defines being human as being created in the image of God. Yuval Noah Harari, our time's astute herald of technocratic visions is merely revisiting Scheler's thoughts when he points out that the US Declaration of Independence is heavily imbued with "religious mythology":

"We hold these truths to be self-evident, that all men are created equal, that they are endowed by their Creator with certain unalienable rights, that among these are life, liberty and the pursuit of happiness."

These words are still the yardstick of good political governance and provide the basic ideals for democratic states everywhere in the world. We all grasp the pathos inherent in these words. But demythologising them proves to be surprisingly difficult.

The outlook for spiritualism's future is bleak. With Kepler or Pascal, who justified their curiosity with their deeply religious belief in God, science succeeded in making dramatic progress, because people like them sought truth for spiritual purposes (*ad maiorem Dei gloriam*). Humanists, Buddhists, etc, have spiritual traditions that were linked with science at all times. But Donald Trump? He considers science as no more than a tool for satisfying human needs – parading, here too, his totally egocentric way of thinking in only the shortest term: Science has to yield profits - for him, his family, the people backing him, the *winners...*

Let's be frank: Why should human beings that computer simulations design as social Darwinists be interested in science? Why should they be social, sympathetic, and "human"? Why should they mind the future of humanity? They are seeking to maximise their benefits (*pursuit of pleasure*) - hence, Donald Trump acts more "rationally" than even the professors of Harvard or the technicians of Silicon Valley when he does just that. Trump embodies the zeitgeist that these people created together with their sponsors from industry and commerce, and yet he has used social media in a totally different way than the one envisaged by their naive creators. Trump showed ingenuity, we would have said in the past. It also means that not everything can be simulated - and that's what we, ironically, call history.The modern age, it is frequently said, is often characterised by the project of subjectivity. *Cogito ergo sum. I* am doing the thinking, it's not someone else doing it for me! But as we find to our surprise, deep inside this "*I*" lies something resembling a more spiritual concept of humanity as well. It's misconceived technology that's giving individuals - from Jane Doe to Donald Trump - the power to change this. Now, they can say: *I* think for myself! *I* am the expert for everything. *I* don't have to listen any more, neither to people nor anything else! And that's the instant in which reality liquefies...

First-Aid Measures and Wrong Expectations

Social media are a social experiment conducted on the largest scale imaginable. Nobody tested them before they were launched, everybody uses them differently and every user re-discovers and revisits them every day. Those who believed social media to be a fringe phenomenon, a type of youth sub-culture we wouldn't have to worry about in our daily lives, found their belief hacked to pieces by the presidential race in the US, during which a candidate won against the united front of the traditional media. Said candidate ignored all the rules of former presidential races and relied exclusively on the power of the social media. Even assuming a benevolent attitude towards the person and the movement of the new President of the US, one can hardly ignore the fact that the world has since become a less predictable and safe place.

How can the destabilising power of the social media be contained? Below please find a couple of first-aid measures:

First of all, e-mail accounts must be protected against attack. And I mean *all* e-mail accounts: those of politicians as well as those of normal citizens. Henceforth, it must be a civic responsibility to use only e-mail accounts that get encrypted on servers. In like manner, government policy must massively promote the use of e-mail encryption. Especially politicians act irresponsibly when they don't encrypt their e-mail. They are endangering not only themselves, but other people as well. The German Basic Law says in Section 10 (1):

"The privacy of correspondence, posts and telecommunications shall be inviolable."

This principle of law must be restored immediately (subject to the limitations of Paragraph 2)!

Secondly, all citizens and especially the members of political parties must be encouraged to get involved on Facebook. Reading newspapers and making a public display of your irritation with the social media won't make a difference as long as you don't have a Facebook account! The battles are raging on Facebook, and there aren't any mitigating forces there. It is a disaster when misrepresentations, propaganda and verbal incendiaries are tolerated without a word of contradiction. Whenever users on Facebook demand in the most aggressive fashion that the President of the Federal Republic of Germany be elected directly by the people and denounce our entire political system as corrupt, an educated person (maybe a social science teacher) should raise his voice and remind people of Hindenburg, the last president of Germany to be elected directly by the people. Where are the theologians and Christian churchgoers when somewhere on Facebook someone derides the Pope by calling him an old moron? Don't they care? How many thousands of students are there reading Islamic studies and Middle Eastern languages? Don't they see what's going on in their Facebook domain, that there is already a civil war going on with words? Why don't they intervene and join the discussion? They possess the knowledge to distinguish between reasonable and unreasonable fears. The situation would be much more relaxed if citizens actually fulfilled their responsibilities in the social media.

Thirdly, Twitter should not be ignored at any time. Twitter redefines the term media power. People wishing to receive balanced news reports need to boost the attractiveness of the public-law broadcasters/media that are present on Twitter and still among the major players there. Political parties of the middle ground need to specifically attract celebrities with a large following.

TO BE HONEST, THERE'S LITTLE HOPE that the social media in their current structure will be compatible in the long term with democracy as we know it. One could of course hope that the better educated strata of society and the political middle ground will form stronger networks with one another in the medium term, which would bring some relief. Yet, given their current structure, I don't understand how the social media should contribute to a functional political middle ground. The entire field of communication and data processing must be put to a rigorous test if our democracy is to be preserved.

No falling back on old recipes! No phoney activism or political platitudes! The rule of law hardly helps in those areas where social media are prone to demagogy. It may be possible to ban the dissemination of hate messages, maybe even Facebook-wide, provided the company Facebook cooperates. But it would be ridiculous to expect much from that, because hate messages get churned out and shared non-stop. When you try to call people to account over their hate messages, you won't find much except the banality of evil. What will you accuse them of? That they put a little edge someone else's comment? Should the 925 people who liked their postings be considered as accomplices and put on trial as well? Have the offenders made their statements in public after all? And what will happen if 2,000 people express their solidarity with the convicted offenders by publishing the offending message again? Will we have to wait for the verdicts of 2,000 court trials? This approach will backfire, exposing the rule of law to ridicule.

Many politicians still live in the world of yesterday. They seriously believe that the political opinion-forming process taking place on Facebook is just more popular with the people and that they would only have to make a stronger effort and give their citizens with better explanations of complex issues. - In their minds, these politicians still stand in a real room in front of a real crowd where they deliver their speeches, only in simple, easily accessible language that copies the way people speak. How far will they go in simplifying politics, how coarse do they want their language to become? Do they really want to emulate the US?

Others are wagging a warning finger and demand an education offensive. People have lost respect, they say, which is why they are so abusive in their treatment of each other in the social media. That's confusing cause and effect again. Respect within society is fading, because people in the social media are growing accustomed to rude language, not the other way round! I'm not denying that respect will always be the right approach. When Katrin Göring-Eckhardt and Frauke Petri treat each other respectfully during a newspaper interview, that's a sign of hope for our society. Both women deserve respect, because I know the kind of scandalous abuse they have to put up with on Facebook. Their exemplary approach to one another has nothing to do with the things their respective Facebook fans write about their respective champion's opponent. The women's action to publicly demonstrate an open mind for the other side is good old politics, though without any impact on the manner of expression in the Facebook comments. Electronic communication follows different rules than face-to-face communication.

Those believing that one might control social media by making changes on the outside, fail to see the opportunities for agitation that social media offer on the inside. In the past, people needed a really loud voice or many other voices to join in if they wanted to shout down a speaker on the microphone. On Facebook, it's enough to just keep posting something at the top-most conversation level to take over an entire group. Where expressed opinions meet with opposition, the opposing views are either simply ignored or countered by two more messages effectively dismissing these other opinions. This way, one individual can hijack a group with thousands of members for his private political campaign.

Originally, political agitation is the domain of dictatorships. That's the reason why autocracies the world over are so jittery about technology that places the means of spreading propaganda in the hands of private individuals. Facebook and Twitter are always close to being shut down in these countries, which, ironically, is a big boost to their reputation as a bulwark of democracy. Then again, no one was quicker to grasp the possibilities offered by this new instrument of power than autocrats.

They rushed to install regional Facebook alternatives that guarantee the government has access to them. The social bots and trolls that everybody is talking about today have in all likelihood been invented as a defensive measure by dictatorial regimes. Now these measures can be deployed to destabilise democratic states. Democracy doesn't have recourse to such tools, exposing them is difficult, debunking a disinformation campaign in real time is virtually impossible. It may be doubted that the involved citizens' initiative alone will be enough to neutralise an organised opponent performing a concerted action.

We should stop trivialising the challenges that social media pose for society! For the first time in post-war history, democracy is fighting for survival and needs to demonstrate its ability to defend itself. That's the reason why we have to draw a clear line between the two faces of social media! The friendly face says: "Why don't y'all talk to each other?" We can find this friendly face in our groups of friends and on innumerable, innocuous Facebook pages where small businesses, schools, museums and parishes present themselves. This is the official face you get in your search results. The other face, the dark shadow of the friendly one, isn't visible until you happen to run into it. Dumbfounded, you stumble over individuals spewing verbal abuse and believe that's nothing new, the problem being that such incidents have recently become more frequent, for "external" reasons. You believe that it will be sufficient to call individuals to account personally. But you are ignoring the fact that the whole stage of agitation, simplification and political defamation on which democracy is gradually being disassembled and pushed into the black hole of dissolution has already been set up.

If you haven't the courage to face this truth and fail to understand that the ambivalence of the social media is an inherent structural problem, you won't be able to respond appropriately. And in that case, no education campaign, no enforcement of the law, no military unit for cybersecurity will be able to do anything effective to protect democracy.

Peace With Facebook & Co?

I *have a running war with the media* – that's a concise statement Donald Trump made on his second day in office, yet he was wrong about even that: this first war he is waging is not a private war. We all find ourselves in an era of war: the social media are waging war against the traditional media, the Twitter and Facebook communities against the real-life societies of peoples, and the social-Darwinist concept of humanity against the spiritual concept of humanity grown out of cultures that each represent a certain mentality.

The US is the world's leader, and again, everything depends on the US. That's why I don't wish to make big speeches about the social media whose future is decided on the other side of the Atlantic Ocean. But I am certain that right now, in the instant I am writing this, there are feverish discussions about the situation going on in Silicon Valley. What went wrong in the social media? What has led to that development? Trump's election to President of the US is a milestone event that's comparable to the Sputnik Crisis, though much larger in dimension and headed in the opposite direction. The Sputnik Crisis showed that US universities had neglected natural sciences and technology, while the

"Donald Trump Shock" is proof that the intellectual culture is corroding, a process that has been going on for decades.

The social media are a gift from the powerful programming languages that were developed in the past decades: PHP, Ruby, Python, etc. They allow programmers to set up Internet platforms with relatively little effort, on which people from all over the world can store information in databases. The process in which the information gets stored is defined by the provider of the respective platform, ie companies like Facebook, Twitter, YouTube, Airbnb, etc.

Internet platforms, by the way, don't require huge computer centres. As long as the number of users is manageable, a single computer will completely suffice, like Mark Zuckerberg's computer, thirteen years ago. Soon, every private citizen may be able turn their computer into a server and offer a privately run platform that provides as many possibilities for social communication as Twitter or Facebook. Essentially, there still exists the basic rule that programmers decide what a platform's design will look like, and the people decide if and how they use the platform. Yet, responsibility in this fast-moving area keeps shifting.

At present, the main responsibility lies with the providers of the large social networks. They are the ones who must ask themselves why this disaster happened in the first place and how they contributed to it. They are also the ones holding the key to defusing this social problem and putting the US back on the democratic track. Because they are the only ones in a position to change the structure of these networks and thereby ensure that the above mentioned basic errors and faults no longer have any effect. So, what are they waiting for? Do they really want to risk damage to the societies of other nations? At present, India's network is too incomplete for social networks to pose any danger, but do they really want to risk that this multi-ethnic nation breaks apart in a civil war? Do they want to tacitly accept that ochlocracies like the one on the Philippines rise everywhere? Or that Europe sinks into war again?

What was the main mistake these companies made when they rushed to bring their social networks to the world so hastily? - It was a clique of technicians at work who had never talked to a humanities scholar. I bet that to this day there are no historians, philologists or political scientists working in any of these companies. No poet ever took a sniff in their respective kitchens and sounded an early alarm that the language used was about to explode into flames. Facebook was not tested by school pupils; there was no evaluation of Facebook performed by prison inmates in a trial supervised by a psychologist; and still, Facebook serves as the arena where billions of people are pitched against each other, no questions asked, and given all sorts of "liberties"!

WHAT WOULD HAPPEN if the social media changed their tack? And what could this change of tack look like?

In a first step, Facebook and other social media would have to state a clearly defined purpose. For some purposes and topics, like fish-keeping as mentioned above, the current Facebook structure is completely adequate. However, groups discussing topics like politics, religion, and international relations need to be managed differently. The principle of anonymity must be abolished for these groups, resumés need to gain relevance, the weighting of opinions must be introduced. Maybe the administrator of a group can define a certain number of people who have the exclusive right of "posting first", while all other members are only allowed to respond to these posts with their comments. Maybe political discussion groups always need to be open groups, maybe the algorithm has to learn how to suggest groups from the opposite end of the spectrum, etc - there are no holds barred concerning Facebook's creativity, but the goal is to reconcile society with what is happening on Facebook.

With Twitter, it would suffice to limit the number of followers each user can have. Such a limit would still allow users to establish an interesting sub-culture, but

Twitter would no longer be saddled with the problem of politics. Also, being allowed to read Donald Trump's diary would then be a privilege again.

In a second step, the social media could focus on their true strengths. Don't these strengths specifically include the realm of the humanities? Isn't collective co-operation and communication specifically interesting in those areas where the social media are failing so dramatically at the moment? Isn't the true nature of these media much closer to the hitherto scorned humanities than the world of technology and commerce?

At present, the entire spiritual and intellectual legacy of humanity is slowly being collected and archived in digital libraries. It is sitting there openly in its many thousand languages, waiting to be tapped for sagacious exploration. If, for example, someone is pondering the term "freedom", he doesn't have to do so in his car in order to initiate a commonplace survey. He can access a database and will immediately find everything humanity ever said about "freedom". In this instance, big-data methods are useful for identifying connections. Who knows how young our modern everyday language and science language, both considered as immutable by technocrats, really are? Who knows that Shakespeare never used the term "revolution" with the meaning it has today? Does "freedom" mean the same thing as the German term "Freiheit"? It may be a bit different...

To cut a long story short, digitisation has significantly increased the possibilities for exploring the intellectual and spiritual history of humanity, for comparing things, and telling right from wrong. Aided by social media, humanity could compile databases, making the knowledge stored there transparent in a way hardly imaginable before.

The work methods employed by Humanities scholars have improved considerably over the past years. But this improvement still lags far behind what utilisation of social media would make possible. Everybody could start their own database, structuring their personal knowledge as they see fit. Then they could start networking to take a look into their colleagues' databases to the extent their colleagues would grant them permission. Researchers could collaborate on highly complex research projects although they are living thousands of miles apart... - Something like that is happening already: think of Wikipedia that's taking this different approach. But what part do companies like Facebook or Twitter contribute to these developments? These companies are raking in billions and have already solved the major technical problems of networked communication with their huge program databases, yet their productive share in advancing the Humanities is nil.

Isn't it tragic that on Facebook uninformed people talk on the most primitive of levels about Islam and let their tempers flare up thinking about the next crusade or the Thirty Thears' War, while somewhere, also on Facebook, two real experts in this field have discussed the exact same topic and didn't delete their postings? Maybe these two true experts would allow us to read their conversation. But Facebook doesn't even know they are true experts, nor does it have any idea that they might be able to help us. This practical connection is never made.

The social media still need to learn a lot in order to develop their true potential. Once their development has taken the right direction, they will be of great service to humanity, and future generations will look back on the problems of our day as though they were the teething troubles of an epochal human invention.

On A Final Note

An essay is a journey in which you travel light, it's just skimming over the tops to get an overview over a broad field. Hence, I have limited my skimming to a few points, with my line of thought based only on what most of my readers already know or experienced themselves. Still, the outcomes surprised even me. With each milestone I reached, with each step I got closer to my destination, my general outlook became gloomier.

I am a Japanologist by profession, I read and analyse ancient texts and also work as a Buddhist priest. True, I wouldn't have felt called upon to tackle a topic like this if the world weren't going up in flames around me. I am not deluding myself: actions are always preceded by thought, and the war of words raging in the social media today may be tomorrow's hot war in the real world.

Increasing scarcity of resources, climate change, unfair terms of trade: all these problems have been well known since the 1980s. However, solutions for these problems have not been found during the fast-paced technological change, they were pushed back to a later date. Today, it is no longer possible to ignore these problems, because too many people are already caught up in the fear of socio-economic decline. Politically correct affirmations no longer help, and lobbyists firmly lodged in the system's every nook and cranny get exposed at regular intervals. There seems to be only one way out, namely use the social media to influence public opinion and indignantly demand that political recipes from the past be applied again. From this perspective, Donald Trump appears to be like Brezhnew, and the social media act like Prawda to capitalism sinking into self-inflicted failure.

As long as we consider what's happening in the social media as an expression of anger (which would be more than justified) we are missing the way they basically function. We get angry ourselves, falling easy prey to those who manipulate our anger and abuse it to feed us disinformation.

Let's be honest and use our unclouded common sense! Alternative truths will be the undoing of humanity. That's the reason we have to fight them at the very place where they are created. I don't believe that any society can afford to continue tolerating a background discourse that spreads so much malice, slander and so many half-truths as the social media do at present.

Anyone seriously wishing for this nightmare to end must advocate a different type of social media: social media that make people more knowledgeable instead of cementing their know-it-all attitude; that promote tolerance and respect instead of mutual contempt; that teach reason and moderation instead of consumption. Is it really so hard to understand that societies don't exclusively subsist on commercialism or socio-economic ranking systems? If those responsible at the social media would grasp what the term "social" means, what the defining features of society are, a structural reform of these media might still be possible. And the perfect time for this would be now.

Recommended Literature

Czeschik, Johanna Christina und Lindhorst, Matthias (et.al.): *Gut gerüstet gegen Überwachung im Web. Wie Sie verschlüsselt mailen, chatten und surfen* (Weilheim: Sybex, 2016)

Eribon, Didier: *Rückkehr nach Reims* (Frankfurt a.M.: Edition Suhrkamp, 2016)

Harari, Yuval Noah: *Sapiens: A Brief History of Humankind* (Vintage, 2014)

O'Neil, Cathy: *Weapons of Math Destruction: How Big Data Increases Inequality and Threatens Democracy* (Random Penguin House, 2016)

Pyta, Wolfram: *Hitler – Der Künstler als Politiker und Feldherr. Eine Herrschaftsanalyse* (München: Siedler Verlag, 2015)

Scheler, Max: *Die Stellung des Menschen im Kosmos* (Darmstadt: Reichl Verlag, 1928)

Schirrmacher, Frank: *Ego. Das Spiel des Lebens* (München: Karl Blessing, 2013)

Seeßlen, Georg: *Trump! Populismus als Politik* (Berlin: Bertz+Fischer, 2017)

Thiel, Peter und Masters, Blake: *Zero to One: Notes on Start Ups, or How to Build the Future* (Crown Business, 2014)

Weber, Max: *Politik als Beruf.* (München und Leipzig: Duncker & Humblot, 1919)

Welzer, Harald: *Die smarte Diktatur. Der Angriff auf unsere Freiheit* (München: S.Fischer, 2016)

www.ingramcontent.com/pod-product-compliance
Lightning Source LLC
Chambersburg PA
CBHW051103250726

48656CB00001B/447